Loving Yourself First

Loving Yourself First

A Woman's Guide To Personal Power

Linda Coleman-Willis

WLW Publishing
10933 Penney Ave.
Inglewood, California 90303
ISBN 1-890368-00-8

Book Design - M Systems - Publishing Group, Los Alamitos, Ca.
Book Cover – Victoria Graphics, Orange, Ca.

Printed in the United States

CONTENTS

Foreword by

Les Brown

Linda Coleman has a strong commitment to the field of motivation and personal achievement. She has worked tirelessly over the ten years I have known her to continue to develop her talents as a speaker. I have watched her grow into one of the top motivational speakers in the country today through sheer persistence and determination.

As I travel across the country speaking, people often approach me and ask for advice and direction on becoming a speaker. Few follow it. Linda is one of the exceptions. She did everything I told her and more. She joined the National Speakers Association (NSA) and has become a viable part of the Greater Los Angeles Chapter. NSA is an association that develops professional speakers. After attending one of my speak for a living seminars held all across the country, Linda produced her first set of audio cassette tapes and sent me a copy. Needless to say they were the same high quality of work I had come to expect from Linda. All of her hard work certainly paid off.

It was only natural that I thought of Linda when the opportunity was presented to me to get involved with personal development television. A project on which Gladys and I worked together. I caught up with Linda in Oakland where she was doing an engagement and I was speaking in San Francisco. We spoke on the phone at 1:00 AM. How many people do you know are excited about anything at 1:00 AM? But, we talked and agreed she would join my group in Los Angeles.

I sat across from Linda last April at the radio station in Los Angeles as her very first guest as she launched her radio talk show, "The Motivation Power Hour." Now one year later the show is a great success and I am writing the forward to her book, "Loving Yourself First." The successes just keep on coming.

Linda has climbed to heights most people only dream about. But all of us have the same power to live our dreams. All of you can achieve if you are willing to do the work. Linda was willing. She is an example of what you can do when you believe in the possibilities for your life. When you are willing to take risks. When you set goals and work to achieve them. When you are persistent, refusing to give up even when things look bleak. It was at my bleakest moments that I had my most profound break through.

All of us have the potential for greatness, but few ever achieve it because few are willing to do whatever it takes. Success is never easy and it seldom comes quick. You have to be willing to go through the rough times in order to enjoy the good times. Keep working to discover your talent. All of us have a talent, a purpose in life. Linda has the ability to inspire and motivate people. That is her gift. What is yours? Don't give up until you have found it.

This book is a guide to self-awareness and self-appreciation. It is for any one wanting to take charge of their life. This book provides clear insights into some of life's most challenging situations and gives you the necessary skills to effectively deal with them.

When you read this book, read with a pen and paper in hand. The ideas and concepts in this book work. They worked for me, they worked for Linda and they can work for you. But, you have to make a commitment to the process. You must do the work. The work I am referring to is the work you must do on yourself.

What is it you want to achieve? What is it you want out of life? Whatever it is, if you make up your mind that you will not be denied you can have it. This book will give you the insight, the motivation and the tools you need to climb the mountain. It is you who must decide whether or not you are going to do it. Remember that it's not over until you win.

Les Brown, The Motivator
Author of *Live Your Dreams* &
It's Not Over Until You Win

Preface

Linda Coleman-Willis has captured on paper her inimitably popular, up-close, personalized style of getting women to see that life is not a dress rehearsal. The curtain comes up once and, when it goes down...it's down. It's what you do between curtains that determines your success or failure, your wealth or poverty of mind and spirit, your love and business relationships and, most importantly, how you feel about yourself.

She gives us a 100-watt flashlight to free ourselves of old baggage, hang-ups and mythical distractions by learning to love and understand who we are. Because many women have been taught that loving oneself is narcissistic, they place love of mother, father, children, grandchildren and even pets above love for themselves.

Coleman-Willis makes the reader see how many illnesses are directly related to how we feel about ourselves. Backaches, headaches, loneliness, depression—if not properly addressed and worked on—will turn inward. And these have been linked by the field of medicine to some cancers, obesity, high blood pressure and heart attacks.

Loving Yourself First proves that you don't have to play the hand you're dealt to stay in the game. It's one of those rare blueprints for how to R-E-S-P-E-C-T yourself—how to get rid of the "need to feel loved" by actually being and becoming loved, how to attract a loving mate, and the four best-kept secrets of personal power. In a journey of self-realization, *Loving Yourself First* is to take the first step to "create the life you want and need." Excuses are history. *Loving Yourself First* is the future.

> Julia Hare, Ed.D.
> National Executive Director, The Black Think Tank
> Author of: *How To Find A BMW (Black Man Working)*

Acknowledgements

In Loving Memory Of My Father

Rev. Matthew L. Brown

To My Husband: You are the wind beneath my sails. You are my best friend. You are the reflection of love I see when I look in the mirror. You are a reflection of me. Thank you for allowing me to be me while still loving me. You are all I could hope for in a partner, and I am so lucky you chose me to be your wife.

To My Mother: I love you and respect you for your great wisdom and strength. You have always stood up and been an example for all of us to follow. It is your strength that has gotten me through, and it is your struggle that has allowed me to become the best that I could be. I thank you for the gift of life, and I thank you for the gift of loving myself.

To My Daughters: I have always loved you, and have made most of my decisions in my life based on that love. The two of you were the reasons I was able to avoid the wrong choices so many of my friends have made. I would think about your dependence on me, and your helplessness, and I would say 'I can't do that because I have two little girls I have to think about.' I did not always make the right decisions, but I always made the best decisions I was capable of at the time. This book is written for you. I hope that something I have written in this book will help you in your time of need, when you are searching for something that can make a difference in your life. I can only assist, and I will do that lovingly and willingly. But, the ultimate responsibility for your life choices is with YOU.

To My Grandchildren: I hope I can always live up to the privilege of being   "Nanna" to all of you. I am proud of you and I want the best of everything for you. You are the reasons I have made such long strides in life. You are my   "Why" for wanting to be successful. My "Why" for wanting to leave a legacy. You are also part of the reason I am writing this book. I hope you will read it one day and it will help you in your quest to love yourself. If I have taught you nothing else, I hope I have taught you to love yourself and, in loving yourself, you can love others.

To My Sisters, and my One and Only Brother: Thank you for being who you are, and allowing me to be who I am. I can't imagine having grown up without all of you in my life. Now that we are all adults, I can tell you how I really feel... *"I Love You."*

SPECIAL ACKNOWLEDGEMENTS

No one writes a book by herself. There are always other people there encouraging, supporting, cajoling, scolding, rejoicing, helping you to get unstuck, reading manuscript— over and over and over again. Without the help of these people, this book would not have happened.

First and foremost, I give thanks to God from whom all creative thoughts flow. Special thanks to my partner, Mr. Welford Willis, III, my friend and confidant. Thanks to James Davis, III (12 years old) for the work he did on helping me with ideas for a book cover. Thanks to Tasha Coleman and Lenee` Willis for your clerical support. Kudos to Dana Mervin for the design and the layout of my book, and for coming through despite impossible deadlines. Thanks to Corliss Tillman for pointing me to Dana, and for your encouragement and support. Your expertise has been invaluable. Thanks to my editor, Helen Bungert. Your expertise has put the finishing touches on an otherwise shaky work of art. Thanks to Janel Stephenson for reading the chapters and doing the exercises. Thanks to Dr. Nina Craft for her support and input.

Then there are those people that every time they see you, they ask you if your book is completed. They are the people responsible for your burning the midnight oil to get it out. Thank you, Les Brown, for asking "Do you have a book...yet?" Thank you, Barbara Lindsey, for planting the seed over and over and over again. Thank you, Dr. Rosie Milligan, for being my resource person and for asking nicely, "How you coming with your book?" Thank you, Debrena Jackson-Gandy, for helping me believe that it really could happen. Thanks to a very special lady, Barbara Wright Sykes, for your counsel, friendship, expertise, and for just being there when I needed a shoulder. Thanks to my radio audiences for asking "When did you say your book is coming out? I want to *buy* a copy." Well, its finally here!!! Thanks to the thousands of women I have spoken to all across the country that inspired this book. Thank you for your stories, your ideas and your support of this book. You are all part of this success story.

Introduction

It has taken me almost a lifetime to realize that the success stories that I have often read are about ordinary people doing-extraordinary things. I used to believe these people were somehow different from the average person, and certainly different from me. It took me a long time to realize that I, an average woman, could also do extraordinary things. If we are not born of wealth or privilege, we tend to believe we are stuck with who we are. My life's experience has taught me that this is simply not true. You can change your life, and you can change it now. All you have to do is be willing to learn what to do, and then do it. That sounds pretty simple, doesn't it? Well, it is simple-when you know what to do.

But, we all have challenges in life that sometimes gets us off track, and we have a difficult time getting right back on. Things happen to us that we are not prepared for. Maybe it's the loss of a job or of a loved one. Life is challenging; so often we are ill equipped to deal with the challenge. This book is written to help you discover the power you have inside. The personal power we all have. But, we have to learn to use it. We are equipped with everything we need to be successful, and to live happy, healthy, productive lives. This book will help you tap into that power.

This book is written by a woman for women. I am not a celebrity, nor did I have a privileged background. But I am a woman, and I have experienced what most of you have. I have struggled with love relationships, raising children, money issues, failed businesses, being over-weight, the death of a loved one, divorce, getting older, and many more of life's complexities. I have experienced the negative effects of doubt, fear, worry and failure. I know first-hand what it is to struggle through life with feelings of being inadequate. We are all in this together.

That is why I wrote this book. To take the complication and mystery out of life's experiences. We can all take charge of our lives, become outstandingly successful, attract the relationships we want and live happy, healthy, productive lives, when we know who we are, and we can accept and love that self.

Over the years I have met lots of women in my seminars. Some of their stories are in the book. These women were of all ages, income levels, social backgrounds, and ethnic groups. All different; yet I found a common theme running through their stories. These women had never learned how to love themselves. They seemed to be forever trying to love and take care of someone else.   Their men, their children, even their parents and friends-at great personal expense. *Loving Yourself First* gives women the permission they need to begin to love themselves first, so that they can love the other people in their lives properly.

This book is for the woman who finally wants to get it right. Who wants to make a change. Who wants to take control of her own life. This book is for all the women out there who have thought about giving up, but held on. This book is for the woman who wants to experience a new and different life. Let us get it right together.

I am writing this book in support of you. I am writing this book in hopes of reaching out to you, and getting you to love and appreciate who you are right now, and what you can become, simply by loving yourself first. Say yes to yourself. Say yes to your life.

This book provides the "what to do" and the "how to do it." You, and only you, can actually do it. So I hope by reading this book you have made a commitment to take action. If you do the work, change will happen.

Loving Yourself First allows women to explore their feelings. It provides clear insight, compassionate understanding and practical solutions. There are exercises at the end of each chapter. Commit to the process. Do the exercises. Keep a journal. Read the book and then read it again. You always get more out of it the second or third time you read it. Share it with a friend-another woman you know who might need it or enjoy it. This book has all the elements necessary to help you change your life. This book is about personal power. This book empowers women. It encourages you to take care of yourself. Trust that you are going to do the right thing. Develop the strength to direct your own life.

Help yourself and become responsible for what you want to happen in your own life. Exercise your body and your mind. Treat yourself like you would your best friend or lover. You deserve it. Take care of your body; it's the only one you have. Pay attention and be aware of what is happening around you. This is your life, your story, and your show. If you don't like it, change it. Make it whatever YOU WANT it to be. Let's grow together. I am pulling for you. I want to help you make a difference in your own life. You can do that by loving yourself first. Then you can help make a difference in other people's lives. But you must **Love Yourself First.**

Because I now accept and love myself positively and unconditionally, I know others will accept me in the same manner.

How To Use This Book

First and foremost, read with an open mind. If you read something that is completely new to you, do not discount it before really thinking about it, and at least giving it a chance to succeed by trying it. Some of the ideas and suggestions you read in this book may be new to you. Perhaps you have never used affirmations or visualization techniques. The explanation of what these techniques are, and how to use them, are included in the exercises at the end of the chapter.

Secondly, do the exercises at the end of each chapter. Keep a notebook or a journal. Keep it with you as you read. Make it your own personal, private book. Respond to the questions by writing the answers in your journal. You will be taking advantage of three learning techniques-reading the information, thinking about it, and writing it down. This totally engages you in the process of learning and helps to reinforce the message. You are also creating an action plan for your life.

As you read the book, it will stimulate your thoughts. It will motivate you to take action. But it is your own excitement and enthusiasm that will compel you to act. Doing the exercises at the end of each chapter can fuel that excitement and enthusiasm. This book is the fuel; you are the engine. Fuel ignites, but it is the engine that creates the movement that gets us going. Working together, they create a spontaneous combustion.

LOVE YOURSELF FIRST and your life will change for the better.

Chapter 1

Loving Yourself First

This title came to me in the middle of the night. I believe it came to me, because it is the message we all need to hear right now. It came to me because I had been thinking of all the problems I've heard women talk about. There was a common thread running through all of these stories. All these women were trying to love someone else, before they loved themselves. Sadly, they did not realize it. I only realized it after hearing the same complaints from women over and over again. They were involved with some guy, and could not figure out why he mistreated them. They were always trying to win some guy's approval or affection. They were always complaining, always dissatisfied. These women were not in the least interested in developing their talents or in getting to know themselves. They were always planning and scheming about how to get a man. I know because I used to be one of them. It was not until I started working on knowing myself, knowing what I wanted in life, knowing what my values and goals were, knowing what I needed and what I had to offer, that my life began to change.

Until we love ourselves, we cannot possibly love anyone else. I know you have heard that a thousand times, but have you ever really stopped to think about what it means? I know what most of you will say. I love myself. I take care of myself.   I exercise, eat right, buy the best perfume and clothes, and I keep myself looking good. But I am talking about inner beauty, not outer appearance. There is so much more to a human being than what we see when we look in the mirror. But, let's look at that image for a moment. Are you really doing what you want to do, or are you doing what this billion dollar cosmetic industry says you should do? When you get up in the morning and look in the mirror, do you truly feel good about yourself, or can you only feel good about yourself after you have put on your makeup? Do you have to have a man in your life to be fulfilled? Do you look to others for approval of everything you do or say or wear, or can you make decisions for yourself, regardless of what others may say or think?

Loving Yourself First was born out of the years of hearing women put themselves down defending their choices in men. I have watched beautiful, capable, intelligent women make the most awful choices you will ever see. I couldn't understand how they could allow these men to control their lives. Men with much less to offer than any of the women had. Men who often physically and mentally abused them. I realized that these women had to learn to love themselves first. Once they learned this very valuable lesson, they would not allow themselves to be subjected to such abuse. When they loved themselves first, they would not allow their children to be subjected to abuse-from inside or outside the home. I mean **really** loving yourself. That requires taking time to get to know who you are. We should be required, say as part of graduation, to spend days, even weeks, with ourselves in some secluded location, and get connected to who we are. We really need to get to know ourselves, and to accept and appreciate ourselves. If there are things we don't like about ourselves, we can change them. When we know ourselves, accept ourselves and love ourselves, then we will receive love and acceptance from others.

It is lack of self-love that causes so much grief in the world. People venting their self-hatred onto others. Parents who abuse their children. Men who abuse their wives. People who inflict pain on other people do not love themselves. You cannot see love through hate, peace through confusion, beauty through ugliness, harmony through discord. We have to practice loving ourselves first, so that we can love other people.

This is about loving yourself, not about hating someone else. Loving Yourself First means that you need to know who you are. It requires that you take that inner journey. Learn what you like and don't like. What you have to offer. Take time to discover your strengths and weaknesses. Learn to accept yourself just as you are, but know if you want to, you can change. But change because you want to, not because someone else requires it of you. Change for all the right reasons. Loving Yourself First means that you are capable of loving someone else. Loving yourself first means you will be able to present a healthy you to others and in turn you will be able to develop healthy relationships.   Loving Yourself First is essential to be able to attract into your life the good things that you want. It is essential to be able to truly love someone else, even your children, properly. Loving yourself first means you will not put drugs, alcohol, or any other unhealthy substance, into your body. Loving yourself first is a must if you are to have a happy, healthy relationship with another human being. Loving yourself first is not about ego, conceit, or selfishness; it is about a true, healthy, respect for one's self.   It is about knowing and appreciating who you are. It is about knowing your strengths and weaknesses, and committing yourself to improvement.   Self-love is so powerful it can help wipe out drug abuse, alcohol abuse, gang violence, teen pregnancy, and hate crimes.   If a child is taught to truly love, accept and respect herself, we could truly have a different world.

I remember growing up in a small town in Texas-just as happy and secure as I could be. In those days, I lived in a segregated (Blacks only) community. I went to a segregated school and a segregated church.   The professionals in my community-doctors, lawyers, teachers, etc.--all looked like me. My only real contact with white people was on those rare occasions when we went downtown to shop or to a movie. In the movie theater, blacks sat in the balcony and the whites sat on the floor of the theater. We never got close to them, but this did not bother me. I didn't understand what it was all about anyway, and besides I liked sitting in the balcony.

My parents and teachers worked hard to instill pride, confidence, and self-acceptance in us. They used to say, *"you have to work harder and be smarter, simply because you are Black."* *"People are going to expect more from you."* They made sure we got the message, and that we were well equipped to compete. It was expected, back then, for parents to visit the classroom. The teachers even visited the student's home at least once a quarter. It was not unusual for parents and teachers to be friends. Three of my teachers lived on my block. I used to baby-sit for two of them. The point I want to make is the value of these relationships to my identity, to my self-confidence, and to my ability to excel.

You see, I never thought about being different racially, because everyone around me was the same color. I was aware there were white people across town, and we did not live together, and we were not supposed to like them, and they were not supposed to like us. But, I never really understood it. I did not know what the sting of racism felt like, until I was 13 years old and going to an integrated school. It was then that I was forced to feel unacceptable and different. It was then that I started to question who and what I was. Being told by someone else how I should feel, or what others thought of me, did not put that sting of racism in my heart. It was first-hand experience that did that. It was not an easy thing to deal with. It hurt a lot.

Fortunately for me, I had a foundation that said racism was a lie. That I was OK. It did not erase the pain, but it did help me to cope. Loving myself first helped me deny the lie that was being told about me everyday in this integrated school. Having a strong foundation, free of racism, helped me to cope when I was faced with it.

Imagine what happens to an individual who has not learned to love herself first. Imagine what goes on in the mind of an individual who feels hatred for herself and everyone around her. That person will probably become destructive, to herself and to other people. I am not suggesting we use racism or discrimination as an excuse for violence. There is never any excuse for violence. But, there is, also, no good excuse that really explains racism to a child. It is impossible to see love through the eyes of hate. Hate effects all of us negatively. That is why it is so important to take responsibility for our own mental well being. Love is a healing power. Loving yourself releases that healing power.

It's easy to blame someone else for your problems. It's easier to look outward, than it is to look inward, for your source of pain. It's easy to find fault with others, rather than finding fault with ourselves. But, if we ever want to truly love ourselves, we have to take that inward journey. We have to be willing to look at ourselves as we really are. It all starts with us. We have to be willing to be honest with ourselves. We have to be willing to admit that we are the problem, and that that problem can be handled, changed, whatever is needed for us to get to that loving self. We have to change before we can expect the world to change.

When we are full of hate, we create a world full of hate. But, when we love, especially ourselves, we create a world full of love. We are creating a loving self. A self that is willing to love us back. That self that looks at the world and everything in it as a miracle. That self that knows that we are a part of that miracle, that we are God's greatest creation. That self that is waiting for you to acknowledge it, so that it can acknowledge you back by loving you unconditionally. **L o v e   Y o u r s e l f   F i r s t** and your life will change for the better.

Learning To Love Yourself

We learn to love ourselves first by spending time alone. We need to learn what it is that we like or dislike. What our values are. What makes us tick. Why we are the way we are. We need that quiet time-to be alone and get inside of our own heads. We need to know ourselves better than we know anyone else, and we can only do that by spending time with us by ourselves. Why is that so hard for people to do? Why is it we spend hours getting to know other people, but won't spend time getting to know who we are?

Is it because we have not been taught to do so, or is it because we may not like what we find? Are we afraid of who we may be, or are we just unskilled in getting to know ourselves? Whatever the reason, self-knowledge is not happening and it should be. Through this book, I am giving you ideas, techniques, methods and opportunities to get to know who you are. I believe by getting to know who you are, you will truly begin to love yourself. I already know that if you love yourself first, you can't help but love life and love living and, yes, love others. You will develop a respect for all life. You will realize the value of life and the role you play in the scheme of it. You will recognize that your life has value and you are valuable. You will learn to respect, love and appreciate life. You will know that you are a miracle. You will know that everything on earth can be replaced but life, and that makes it precious, priceless and valuable. When you realize you are a precious, priceless, valuable human being, you will begin to value yourself and others and find a new excitement for life.

You will understand why it is necessary to learn to love yourself before you can hope to love another. Loving yourself first is not about being selfish, it is about being unselfish. It is about being your best self and, therefore, able to share that best self with other people. After all, don't they deserve your best self? You see when we are our worst, we attract the worst of others, but when we are our best we attract the best of others. Loving yourself first is totally an unselfish act. It is only through loving ourselves that we can learn to totally and unselfishly love another. When we love ourselves, we have no trouble loving someone else. I believe this is so important that it is worthy of being a goal for every individual.

Let's play pretend for a moment. Pretend you were the only person on earth. What kind of relationship would you have with you? I suggest you have that relationship with you right now. Try being along with yourself for a period of two days or two weeks, whatever you can spare. Spend this time alone, no television, no radio, no books, nothing but you and your journal. Talk to yourself. Think about the things that are really important to you and ask yourself why? Answer the questions at the end of this chapter. Record everything in a daily journal. Write down everything you do, say or think. This exercise is so powerful. It will reveal things about yourself you never knew. The most important step here is to be honest with you. Remember if you find something that you don't like work on changing it. So, go ahead, be brave. Take that inward journey. See what you find. You may be surprised. It is worth the time and energy to get to know who you are, and to learn to love who you are. It will change your life. You will learn to value yourself more and to listen to yourself more. You will become clear as to what is important in life and what is trivial pursuit.

You should leave this exercise with a new attitude, a renewed zest for life and living. If you really explore the inner beauty you possess, it will change your life forever. You will meet the Godliness in you, the goodness in you, the things that you tend to cover over by trying to fit into a world that tells you what you should be. Don't try to become someone you're not, living a life you have no control over. This exercise puts the control where it belongs-with you. It teaches you to love yourself first. It puts you in touch with what is really important. It helps to clarify life's mysteries. This is one of the greatest challenges you will ever face. But, the rewards are worth it.

You see loving yourself, truly loving yourself, is what God planned. You came here loving yourself first. When you cried as a baby, you were first. Whenever you felt the need to be fed, changed, or held you cried out-me first, me first. It was ok then, and it is ok now. The big difference is then your parents took care of you; now you must take care of yourself. When you cry out for something, you should be the first one to respond. It is you that should hear the cries first. It is you who should know what the cry means and respond accordingly. Your parents were there temporarily. Now it is your responsibility to answer your own needs. When these needs can be met by your own self, then when you interact with another person, whose needs are also being met by her/his own self, then you can come together harmoniously, and share yourself with that person, and not feel needy and unloved and looking to him to fill you up. Love yourself first, and loving another will be easy. Loving yourself first is the natural order. If you don't love yourself first, you are incapable of loving another. You can pretend, but your lack of self-love will intrude on your life sooner or later. The easiest first step, ok, the not so easy first step, is to love yourself first. Try it, you may like it, and even better than that, it works.

EXERCISE

Think about these questions, the answers will help you to get to know yourself better. If you don't know the answers, how can you expect anyone else to?

What makes you happy?
What makes you sad?
What gets you excited?

Write out the answers to the following questions: (answering these questions will help you get to know more about who you are inside).

How well do you know yourself?

What are your values?

What do you want out of life? Why?

Why do you make the choices you make in your personal life? (don't settle for *"I don't know"* or *"because I want to."* Dig deeper to find the why.)

How do you make decisions?

How do you choose your friends? Relationships?

What is important to you?

If your life is not working, what part are you playing in it? (Be honest with yourself)

Who Is Responsible?

What kind of world do we live in? One woman steals a baby to keep a man (the Baby Alex case). She was his mistress and thought if she had a baby for him she could keep him. Another woman killed her babies to keep a man (Susan Smith). A 17-year-old steals another woman's baby in an attempt to keep her boyfriend--after having walked around with her stomach stuffed with a teddy bear for nine months.

What do these women have in common? They were all trying to keep or please a man. In their minds, they saw these acts as demonstrations of love. Love for whom? Themselves? No, love for a man. But, how could something like this happen in a civilized society? Who is responsible? How can a mother put her children in a car and push them in the river and let them drown? It shows just how far we have strayed. These women committed terrible crimes in the name of love. One thing we know for sure, they did not love themselves and were incapable of really loving anyone else, even their children.

All women desire love and affection. Therefore, we must examine ourselves closely, and determine effectively what path to travel so we do not venture on a course of self-destruction.

Loving yourself first must become a habit like all other habits. Habits are formed by doing and doing and doing, until it becomes second nature. Once something becomes a habit, you don't have to think about it. It is automatic. It becomes a way of life. It comes naturally. It should be as natural as breathing.

Why should someone else be more important to us than we are to ourselves? When we are trying to love someone else, with no self-love present it's like trying to squeeze toothpaste from an empty tube. It's empty. You can't get what's not in there. You soon tire of the effort, because the return is not worth the energy spent, and the object is discarded. That is what happens in a relationship when one person does not love herself. The other person tires of carrying the relationship, and expending energy that is not, cannot, be returned and discards the relationship. The person who does not love herself is left hurt and broken and wondering WHY? There is nothing healthy about this type of relationship. But, this person will repeat this scenario over and over again, either with the same person or with others. She will blame other people for her disappointments. She can't or won't see the part she plays in the relationship. She can't or won't take any responsibility for what happened in that relationship, and therefore she repeats the same mistakes over and over again. Of course, she didn't do anything, to cause the demise of the relationship. She did everything right.. She gave her all. She can't understand how anyone could treat her this way.

She is blind to the fact that she did not, could not love anyone else fully, because she was not loving herself fully. Are you at least willing to give to yourself what you are willing to give to the relationship? Are you taking care of your own needs first, or are you looking to a relationship to do that for you? If you enter into a relationship looking to the other person to heal you, you are setting yourself up for disappointment. I know you have always heard two halves make a whole, but in a relationship it takes two wholes to make a whole. We come together in a healthy relationship to complement one another, not to remake each other. The sum total of two parts makes a whole. If one part is broken, the entire object is broken, and unable to function. That is why it is a bad idea to go into a relationship trying to change or fix the other person. First of all, that person has to be interested in being fixed. Then, that person has to take responsibility for fixing himself just as you have to take responsibility for fixing yourself. It is a losing battle, especially if that person does not see the need to be fixed.

So your focus has to be on loving yourself and attracting into your life a healthy partner who loves himself and the two wholes will come together to make a healthy wholesome partnership.

Ladies, it is not so hard to love yourself first, once you understand how important it is and began to practice it daily. Do the wonderful things for yourself that you would do for him. Treat yourself like you would treat him. Take care of yourself, like you take care of everybody else. Value yourself and your time, the same as you would value his time. Decide what you want in a relationship before you enter it. Be realistic about what you have to offer, and understand we attract what we are, not what we want. If you want to be loved, you have to be loving. If you want a healthy relationship, you have to be healthy-both mentally and physically. You cannot look to the universe to give you what you are not giving yourself.

The first step in loving yourself is accepting yourself just as you are, and appreciating that self just as it is. You have the ability to change if you don't like who you have become. In fact the only thing you have complete control over is yourself. You cannot change anyone else, but you can change yourself. Work on you. Get counseling if you need it. Ask for help. When we are ill, we see a doctor. When we have a toothache we see a dentist. So when we are hurting emotionally, we may need to see a therapist.

Read the books, listen to the tapes, take the classes, and go to the seminars. Do whatever you have to do to make you better. This is an investment in your future. Whose life is it, anyway? No one else is going to be responsible for your life, even if you wanted him to. You have to be responsible for your own life. That means healing yourself if you are sick. You can be healthy physically and still be sick mentally. Everyone is so concerned with the outward appearance that they tend to overlook the inward. It is that inward journey that is going to make us whole. That is the hardest part, because we cannot see it or touch it . But we can see it with our minds. This requires use of our imagination and visualization. Imagine every day what you want your life to be like. Use visualization exercises to see it. If this becomes your practice, you will see your life change. I can guarantee it because it happened for me. But, until we are willing to meet ourselves right where we are, we will never get any further. Denial is your worst enemy. It's always someone else's fault. It is never your fault. We are victims. If you play the role of the victim, this means you are helpless to do anything about your situation. I don't believe this. We can always improve our situation by improving ourselves.

Victim is a state of mind. We see ourselves as helpless, as not having a choice in the matter. We did not choose to be victimized, but we choose whether or not we are going to remain a victim. You see a victim is what is left after the violent act, whether mental or physical, is over. Once the act is over, it is our decision whether or not we are going to continue being a victim. I know it is not easy, and maybe we need to seek professional help, but, keep in mind it is not automatic that we have to roll over and become a victim of someone else's act. We can choose not to be a victim. In fact we must choose not to be a victim, or we will always be a victim. When you love yourself, that self-love will not allow you to remain a victim.

I know things happen to us that are out of our control. I know people perpetrate crimes against other people everyday. This is victimization, but I still believe that we do not have to remain a victim. It's not what happens to us in life, but how we respond to it. How we get on after it has happened, after it's over. What we do about what has happened to us. It is about accepting whatever it is and getting past it. Again, I know this is not always easy, but it is always our choice how we decide to handle it. Some people get stuck and never get past it. Others seem to take whatever life dishes out, and keep moving forward.

EXERCISE

If you could have any type of life you wanted right now, what would your life look like? Describe your life avoiding discussion of material things or outer appearances. Tell me what your life would feel like, in terms of characteristics and values. For example: My life would be full of fun and joy. I would have lots of self-confidence. I would have a positive, optimistic attitude. I would only have positive, supportive people around me, etc. Now write out your own description of what your life would look like:

_____
_____
_____
_____
_____
_____
_____
_____
_____
_____

Visualization is using your imagination to see something before it happens. Seeing it in your own mind. Imagining it to be true even if you don't fully believe it yet. We use our imagination all the time. Unfortunately most people use it to imagine the worst. When we worry about something that has not happened, we are using our imagination to predict the future. You can learn to control your imagination, through visualizing good things happening to you. Some people call it daydreaming. Try it. Close your eyes and visualize your perfect day. Where are you? What are you doing? Who are you with? How do you feel? Open your eyes and write a short paragraph describing your perfect day.

My Perfect Day:

_____

_____

_____

_____

_____

_____

_____

_____

_____

_____

Affirmations are sayings or beliefs that empower us to keep moving forward. We repeat affirmations to train our subconscious mind to believe them and react accordingly. If you are spiritual, use some quotes from your source of inspiration. Some examples of affirmations are:

> *I have good work ethic.*
> *I am respectful of other people and myself.*
> *I love myself unconditionally.*
> *I am a seeker of peace and harmony in my life.*
> *I only speak to encourage and edify.*
> *I have courage and determination.*
> *I only attract good, positive people into my life.*

Exercise Your Body And Your Mind

Our health is the most important thing we possess. If we gain the world and lose our health, we don't have anything. We have to take care of ourselves. Exercise at least three times a week. Do something moderate. It does not have to be strenuous. Walk in the mall if you like window-shopping. I run up and down the aisles in the grocery store with a basket full of groceries. I go down every single aisle, whether I want anything from that aisle or not, just to get the exercise. I park far away from the grocery store, so I have further to walk. I walk up escalators and stairs every chance I get. Do anything to get extra exercise, but get it. Wash the car, mow the lawn, and clean the house to a jazz record, any music that will make you move and groove to the beat. Stand up while watching television, so you don't get too comfortable and end up in one position all evening. Put up a basketball hoop in the yard. Yes, ladies, we can go out in the yard and shoot hoops by ourselves if we have to. Invite your favorite girl friend or guy friend over to shoot hoops with you. Try it, you may like it. I certainly do.

If you hate exercise, take up dance. Square dance, or line dancing, ballet, tap, any kind of dancing you enjoy. Don't knock it until you have tried it. Square dancing and line dancing are fun and you use up lots of energy. Ballroom dancing uses up lots of energy also. Exercise gives us energy. The more energy we have the more we feel like doing, and the more healthy activities we do, the healthier we are. Nutrition is just as important. I don't want to preach, but we have to know that we are what we eat. If you want a healthier you, eat healthier meals. Learn how to prepare food you like that is low in fat. Do not diet. Dieting doesn't work. Change your lifestyle. Create a lifestyle that reflects who you are. Don't live to eat, but eat to live. I know this is easier said than done. Most people have had to struggle with their weight at some point in their lives. But, it is not a losing battle if we learn to listen to our bodies and only eat when we are hungry. Don't let yourself get too hungry before you eat, because then your resistance is low and you will eat whatever you can find. Plan your meals and work your plan. Don't be too hard on yourself if you don't get it right the first time. Most of us don't. This is a lifetime work, but your life and good health are worth it. Love yourself just as you are, and you will become what you want to become. Don't put yourself down if you are overweight. Lots of people are overweight. This is not an excuse, but it is the truth. Accept yourself just as you are right now, and work at becoming what you want to be.

Before you can lose weight and keep it off, you have to love yourself. You can love it off, by loving who you are and loving every part of whom you are. Love every ounce of fat on your body, and then choose to release it when you are ready. Don't hate any part of your body, because that is part of who you are right now. It does not have to be who you are tomorrow, next week, or for the rest of your life. Release the weight if you want to, but love who you are with or without it. Never ever say *"I hate my body."* We can't be healthy hating our bodies. We don't take care of things we hate. We don't cherish things we hate. Say *"I want to release some of the weight I have on my body."* But love yourself . Love all of you. Love yourself, regardless of what your body looks like. It is healthy to love yourself. It is a must for a happy, healthy life. I encourage you to adopt this philosophy and live by it.

No matter how overweight you are, love who you are and release the unwanted weight. Do whatever you can, on whatever level you can. Do it and keep looking ahead to what can be instead of what is. Plan for a better body and a healthier life style and don't put yourself down. You do know you have to do something different in order to get different results. So make a commitment to yourself, that you are going to love yourself first, and release the weight second. Once you love yourself, value yourself and appreciate who you are, releasing the weight will be easier.

Allow me to share with you, something that has worked for me, for many years. Have you ever noticed, that people who are stiff, look much older than they really are? Stiffness of the spine has less to do with age than you may think. There are lots of young people with stiffness of the spine. Here is a suggestion that helped me, and perhaps it can help you.

Warning: If you have a medical problem, back or neck injuries, get your doctor's permission before trying any exercise.

The miracle exercise, (as I call it) is yoga. If you have never tried yoga, you are in for a pleasant surprise. You can perform yoga at any age. It is not how well you execute the positions, but how often. The goal is to stretch and strengthen. Yoga helps to limber up your body. If you notice, people who are limber appear younger than they really are. (Now you know my secret). I have practiced yoga for years. Adopting a yoga regimen will help to improve, your concentration, breathing, muscle tone and firmness. It also provides an overall feeling of youthfulness and well being.

There are different types of yoga. I practice *Hatha Yoga* (physical). The objective of Hatha Yoga is to achieve self-realization. Therefore, it is important to concentrate fully on the postures or positions as you perform them. I use Richard Hittleman's 28-Day Exercise Plan. It is a step-by-step guide to yoga positions from the very simple to the more complex. You begin slowly and move at your own pace. You can benefit tremendously from these exercises, even if you never achieve the more complex positions. In a few weeks you will see and feel the difference. Try it, what do you have to lose? Perhaps a few pounds and some stiffness of the joints.

This is the only place in the book where we will discuss the physical. But it is so important, I felt it necessary to include it. I also want to mention **exercising the mind**. Reading, writing, crossword puzzles, playing word games, meditation, prayer, visualization exercises, speed-reading, and memory lessons. Keeping the mind active is as important as keeping the body active.

Loving Yourself and Attracting a Loving Man:

You will know if a man loves himself in a healthy way because you will experience a healthy relationship. When you have a healthy love for yourself, you will not tolerate anything less from anyone else. People can tell when a person loves herself. Men who are looking for women whom they can take advantage of and mistreat, know what to look for. They are looking for a certain type of woman. They say they can spot her a mile away. They can easily tune into her insecurities, because of their own insecurities. This is why it is so important that you work on yourself before you get into a relationship. You bring everything into that relationship with you. Relationships are two histories coming together, yours and his.

If you are unhealthy emotionally, and he is unhealthy emotionally, there is no way you are going to have a healthy relationship. That is like putting a rotten egg into stale cake mix and, just because you put it in the oven you expect it to come out a freshly baked cake. It may look like a freshly baked cake, but the moment you cut into it, you will discover it is rotten to the core. We try to use relationships to fix what is wrong in us. But, we have to learn to fix what is wrong in (and notice I said in, not with) us, **before** we enter into a relationship. Whatever is wrong going in, will continue to be wrong and, chances are, it will be compounded by whatever problems your partner brings into the relationship. In this case $2 + 2 = 5$.

Some women get a man and pour all of themselves into the relationship before they know if he is the right one. You must examine where you are emotionally in your own life. If you are all messed up, you will probably not attract someone who has it all together. We are talking emotionally, because we know we can all put on a good front.

We can cover up a multitude of sins with expensive clothing and a mask. But understand, good clothing does not cover up bad character. Sooner or later we have to face who we are, expressed through our lives. If you want to know who you really are, take a look at your life. If it is all screwed up, then we have to assume there is a problem somewhere. You can continue to look to the outside for the problem if you want. You are only fooling yourself. Your life is a reflection of you, and where you are right now in your emotional growth. Is it a reflection of what you really want or are you settling? If it is not a reflection of what you want, then you know you have work to do. You have to work harder on yourself than you do on anyone or anything else. Your life will not change unless you change. You cannot change other people, but you can change yourself. You can attract into your life the kind of person you want by **becoming** the kind of person you want to be. In fact you must become the person you want before you can attract that kind of person to you. We are talking about character, values and emotions, not outward appearance or material possessions.

You have to develop in character to attract a man of good character. Opposites may attract in personality, but like attracts like in character. If you don't like who you are, know that you have the power to change.

EXERCISE

Answer the following questions about your relationship:

What is it you bring to the relationship, Good? Bad?

Are you being realistic about what you bring to the relationship?

Would you like to be in a relationship with you? Why?

What is it you want from the relationship?

What are you willing to give to get it?

Are you willing to become the person deserving of the things you want?

What's Emotion Got To Do With It?

Women tend to run off emotion. We are the romantic dreamers of the world. Some men are, too. But for the most part, men discover a lot earlier that the fairy tales are not true. Most of you know that men and women are different (of course you are aware of the biological differences). But, men and women are different in other ways, too.

I want you to think for a moment about the person in your life right now. Think back to when the two of you first met. Think about how he made you feel. Remember, everything was so wonderful. The moon was brighter, the air was fresher, and you were in love. Then you had to get to this thing called communication. You had to talk to each other. That's when all the trouble started.

You were both speaking the same language. But, you soon discovered that even though you were both speaking English, you were definitely not speaking the same language at all. As a matter of fact, you had no idea what language your partner was speaking. What happened? Well, the biggest difference between men and women   (excluding biological differences) has little or nothing to do with genetics, but with something called conditioning, learned behavior.

Men and women are taught to see the world differently, to think differently and to interpret things differently.   It's a miracle we can communicate at all, and, if it weren't for biology, we probably wouldn't.   Let's look at some of the differences in our conditioning. Parents tend to place more demands on little boys than on little girls, expecting them to be more responsible and to take more risks.   Parents push little boys to be independent, little girls to be dependent.   They offer less comfort to sons than to daughters when the children are frightened or injured.   They give boys greater freedom at an earlier age than they do girls.   They encourage boys to control their emotions and girls to express theirs. Perhaps that is worth repeating.   Parents tend to encourage their sons to control their emotions (*big boys don't cry*)   and encourage little girls to express theirs (*show me where it hurts.*)

Men are generally shown as authoritative, knowledgeable, macho, even super human like those commercials featuring top athletes, such as Michael "Air" Jordan. (Some men actually believe he *is* super-human).   Women are usually cast in dependent, submissive and weaker roles.   They are the stars, we are the co-stars.   It is changing a bit, but not much.   As a result of this conditioning there are myths surrounding both sexes. Let's take a look at some of these truths and myths:

Truths And (*Myths*)

Men are solution & goal-oriented/Women are process-oriented
(men are hard-nosed stuffed shirts/women scatter-brained)

Men internalize their thinking/Women think out loud
(men are closed-minded/women talk too much)

Men internalize their complaints/Women complain out loud
(men are uncaring/women are naggers)

Men are conditioned to stay in their heads/Women in their hearts
(men are cold, unemotional/women are too emotional)

Men define themselves primarily from their work/Women from relationships
(men are insensitive/women are too sensitive)

Men are more right brain-Visually oriented
(This will explain why he has to LOOK)

Women more left brain-Verbally oriented
(This explains why she has to TALK)

After previewing this list, is it any wonder men and women have challenges communicating? There are lots of good books and seminars on male/female relationships. It is probably a good idea to attend a seminar, or read a few books, so you can understand the differences between men and women, which create so many of the problems we have.

My main focus in this book is on women. But, again, it is important for us to understand the differences between men and women. As you now understand, conditioning has a lot to do with why we communicate so differently. Why our expectations in life, and particularly in relationships, are so different. Do you understand why it is so important for both parties in the relationship to work at understanding how the other person processes information? So many relationships are destroyed because the parties cannot communicate with each other. Women are more likely than men to attend a relationship seminar. So, once again, you may be expected to do most of the work. I am providing you with some relationship strategies to help you. I don't believe you should be responsible for making the relationship work all by yourself. That is impossible, anyway. It takes two. But, perhaps, you will feel confident taking the lead sometimes instead of always being led. Hopefully, this information will help you feel more comfortable asking for what you want in a relationship, or getting out of a relationship that is unhealthy. You are in control. That does not mean controlling another person, it means controlling you. Identifying what you want. Understanding what you bring to the relationship. Being realistic about your expectations. Not over-reacting to every little thing that happens as if it is the end of the world.

(emotions) We cannot always help how we feel, but we can always control what we think and how we act.

Relationship Strategies

1. Work at new ways to communicate.
2. Don't fake or pretend.
3. Don't assume you know what your partner wants-ask him. Don't assume you know what your partner is going to say. Listen.
4. Ask for support in a non-demanding way.
5. Get rid of unrealistic expectations.
6. Learn what your partner's needs are and give him what he needs, but don't sacrifice or forget about yourself in the process.
7. Help your partner become aware of your needs.
8. Take responsibility for getting your own needs fulfilled from a variety of sources. Don't make your partner the source of your dissatisfaction or sole source of fulfillment.

Chapter 2

What's Love Got To Do With It?

What's love got to do with it? Everything. Especially when we are talking about self-love. Loving yourself unconditionally. You can love yourself unconditionally and be in love with another person. I believe you *have* to love yourself unconditionally, before you can truly be in a healthy love relationship with another person. Notice, please, I said *healthy* love relationship. Not all love relationships are healthy. If you love yourself, and he loves himself, it is easy for you to love each other. If you accept and value yourself, and he accepts and values himself, it is easy for you to accept and value each other. This is a healthy whole. Both parties must participate fully. I'm not saying that you both have to feel the same thing at the same time all the time, but if you share core values, then you have a healthy relationship.

We are always going to have challenges in life. So to be able to weather the storms of life, we need to have core values intact. The winds can toss about a strong ship on the sea, but it will move with the sway of the wind and eventually complete its sail. A weak ship will be destroyed by the same winds on the same sea. So it is within the sea of life. We have to make ourselves strong and whole as individuals, so when we become part of something, it is also strong and whole. Love yourself and the world will love you. Love yourself first and you will attract a loving relationship. You have to, because there will not be room for any other kind. A round peg cannot fit into a square shape.

God so loved the world he gave his only begotten son. Whosoever believeth in him shall not perish, but shall have everlasting life. If God loved us so much, and wanted the best for us how can we settle for less? How can we love ourselves less? We are God's greatest creation, his greatest miracle. He created us in his likeness. We should love ourselves as our father loved us.

Life is the most priceless and precious gift we will ever have. Yet, lots of people spend it foolishly. They lose their lives over little or nothing because they place little or no value on it. An automobile, a coat or a ring, has become more important than a human life. We spend billions of dollars to protect things, inanimate objects, while we step over human beings in the streets every day. Something is wrong with this picture. We fight wars to protect things that can be replaced, and, in those wars, we lose the one thing that can never be replaced--life. We lose thousands of lives protecting things that are essentially worthless in the final analysis. The laws protecting things are more important than the laws protecting life. What happened? Where did it all go wrong? When did we stop loving ourselves? When we stopped appreciating who we are and what we represent. We have forgotten what's really important. A human being can be locked away for life for taking an inanimate object, but serve less time if he takes someone else's life. What a message we are sending. It is understandable why some young people do not value life. Life is the one thing we have no control over, the one thing we can never replace, and we take it for granted. Life is a precious gift that is on loan to us and we treat it with great disrespect. We have not come to stay. This thing we call life as we know it will one-day pass away. Yet, we have the opportunity to live it to the fullest and we don't take that opportunity. We are overly concerned with material possessions, and forget what life is really all about. We have forgotten why we are here, and we have forgotten how to love ourselves. We are loving everything and everybody but ourselves.

It is self-destructive not to love yourself. If you do not love yourself, you can destroy yourself or allow yourself to be destroyed by outside forces. It requires great love of self to exist in this world, which places too little value on human life. We must believe that our own lives are important, before we can convince someone else that our life is important. If we believe life and living are important, we will not put ourselves in a situation that could cause harm to us, nor will we be likely to harm anyone else. Teaching self-love is a must. When a human being looks at another human being, that person should be able to see her own reflection. But, too often, we see hate instead of love.

"Gee, I can't believe I did that..."

"She is a well-educated, brilliant woman caught up in an affair with a younger man. He wasn't just younger, he also had a drug problem. She knew intellectually that he was no good for her, but emotionally she wasn't so rational. She lost it every time she saw him. He lives with a woman. She knew that, but it didn't matter. In fact, this brilliant woman has been known to sneak around in the dark, peeking through the windows of his home. He calls her only when he needs money for drugs. They make wild, passionate love and then he is gone... until the next time."

"She was committed and dedicated. She loved her man. In fact, he was the only one for her. Yes, she was in love, and she would do anything for him. Didn't matter that the feeling was not mutual. She had his son. She just knew he loved her. He didn't have to tell her; she could feel it. It was only when he was drinking that he was mean. When he became ill and almost died, it was she who nourished him back to health. She loved him and gave him her all. After he was back on his feet again, and long gone, she could not stop talking about what she did for him. She could not understand how he could leave her after everything she did for him. She became very bitter and eventually started drinking and using drugs herself. She died in her sleep. She never got over being deserted by the man she loved."

"She was beautiful, intelligent, successful, every man's dream. He was tall, dark, handsome, every woman's dream. They met, fell in love, and became inseparable. In fact, they were so inseparable she stopped seeing her friends and family. She *could not accept telephone calls. She could, however, go to work. It became increasingly hard to hide the bruises and the occasional busted lip. She always had an excuse. It was never his fault. It probably would have continued but she ended up in the emergency room after she tried to run away from him and he had thrown her down the stairs, breaking her arm. Her young son tried to help her and was also beaten. Her daughter ran to the neighbors for help. She could not deny, this time, that she had been physically assaulted. She had to face it. He was gone anyway. He did not want to go to jail... again."*

"Is there such a thing as a "bad girl?" Perhaps not, but you can't prove that by examining her life. She has been in the streets since she was thirteen. She left home to get away from her mother's boyfriend. Now the streets have claimed her as one of their own. She earns her money as a hooker. She steals her clothes and food and does whatever she has to do to survive. She feels she doesn't have a choice. She is now 22 years old but doesn't have any marketable skills... well, almost no marketable skills."

"She is smart, pretty, stubborn and self-righteous. She has all the answers, knows everything. She has so much potential. Potential only counts if we recognize we have it. She doesn't seem to notice. She works hard, wears designer clothes, expensive cologne. Her hair and nails are always done just right. Her home is spotless. She drives a nice car and it's paid for. She is attracted to men who are untidy, unemployed, unhappy, needy, greedy and dishonest. She loves to be needed and she is... in the beginning. It never lasts. They get everything they can from her; then they are gone. She drinks, becomes hostile and depressed, until the next one comes along

and it starts all over again. She is aware there is a problem, but says she can't help it; she likes the... "bad boys."

"She is slick. She looks good and talks a good game. She only wants one thing from them, their money. They seem to know it and are willing victims. She insults them, stands them up, occasionally hangs up in their face, but they keep coming back for more. Days pass, sometimes weeks, before she sees them, but when she calls, they come. It's a game to her. Use them up, throw them away. She will never admit it, but she is lonely, insecure and afraid. So she continues this charade, until she begins to disrespect herself almost as much as she disrespects them..."

These are true stories about real women. But, they all have one thing in common. They are stories about women who did not love themselves. They may argue this point, but the proof is in the pudding. In other words, the proof is evidenced by how they are, or in some cases were, living their lives. These are not the actions of women who truly love themselves. Some of these women were very successful, very well educated, very attractive, from great family backgrounds, and had lots of money.

So we know that their actions are not necessarily a reflection of their social or economic status. Why would these women act this way, or allow themselves to be treated this way?

Many women feel they are unworthy if they don't have a man. They worry that they are inadequate or worthless. They harbor fears that they are not good enough. They secretly believe they don't deserve success and happiness and they simply have not been taught to love themselves.

Women tend to define themselves by their relationships. If we are not in a love relationship, we feel worthless. Unfortunately these women found themselves in the wrong relationships. They were drawn in by idealism instead of realism. They allowed their emotions to get in the way of their good sense. When we are in love, good sense is the first thing to go. That is why it is so important to love yourself before you enter into a relationship.

Too often we enter relationships for the wrong reasons. To escape loneliness, responsibility, failure. Or we believe a relationship will fix us. Unfortunately the wrong choice in a mate often leaves us feeling less valued. Neediness makes us vulnerable, and creates dependency on the other person. Chances are very good that that person will have the same challenges we have or greater challenges. They cannot give us what we need, because they don't have it to give. We find ourselves locked into a destructive relationship, unable to get out. If you are not healthy emotionally, you will probably not attract someone who is healthy emotionally. If he is emotionally healthy why would he want someone who is not?

These statements are not meant to downplay the importance of a good relationship, or to disrespect men in any way. There are a lot of good men out there. But, this book is not about men. It is about empowering women. Helping women to develop personally so that they can take charge of their lives and select healthy, loving, supportive men to share their lives with.

So if you are feeling that you need a man to validate you, to make you feel worthy, whole, and cared for, you need to seek guidance and counsel. Sometimes self-help books are not enough. Look for a good therapist or go to your spiritual leader. I have some referrals listed in the back of this book. If you don't heal yourself emotionally, you will probably not be happy, no matter how much success you experience. Too many women neglect their emotional health. We pretend to be strong, competent, fearless women, and inside we are little girls. Little girls nourishing all kinds of hurts, disappointments and abuses. Little girls whose fairy tale did not come true and they are crushed because of it. Little girls who have been let down by men, perhaps even their own fathers.

But, it doesn't matter what has happened up until this point in your life. My question for you is, what are you going to do about it? Are you going to continue getting into relationships that are not emotionally satisfying, unhealthy and destructive, or are you going to do something about it? Are you willing to take that inner journey of healing and peace? Are you willing to admit that there is a problem, and look for solutions, or are you going to stay in denial? Denial is a dangerous thing because, as long as we deny the existence of a problem, we continue to repeat the same mistakes over and over again.

Does this sound like you? Have you gone from one bad relationship to another? Are you going to continue in this madness, or are you going to get back to some semblance of sanity? Are you willing to admit you need help and then seek it?

The woman dominated by need will always be dependent on someone else. But, the woman motivated by desire to be a better person, to live a happy, healthy life, to create balance in her life, to allow a man to enhance her life instead of rule it, to set her own goals and achieve them, to set standards for her relationships, and to love herself first, will always be in charge, even when she is in a good, loving supportive relationship.

She will attract into her life a man with the same character, values and ideals. They will come together to create a healthy, happy, wholesome relationship. I hope this is what you want. I hope this book can convince you that is the only way to live.

We all have emotions. Some negative. Some positive. We cannot always control our emotions, how we feel, but we can control what we think and how we act. What we do. Knowing this empowers you. But, putting this knowledge into practice releases your real personal power.

You can learn to use restraint, logic and reasoning to manage yourself in any situation. This kind of discipline can put you in control of your emotions, thereby putting you in control of your life.

EXERCISE

Repeat these affirmations three times a day. First thing in the morning, in the afternoon, and last thing before you go to sleep at night.

>*"I am in control of my life."*
>*"I can help the way I think and act."*
>*"I will always act in my own best interest."*

Focus on what you want in your life, not what you don't want. Write at least a paragraph (more if possible) describing the kind of life you want:

_____
_____
_____
_____
_____
_____

Focus on actions you can take immediately, even small ones. What can you do today to move you closer to what you want? Identify at least one action step and make a commitment to do it within the next 24 hours. **Action Step:**

_____
_____
_____
_____
_____

Beware: The Romance Trap

I can't tell you how many women I personally know who have let go of good relationships with wonderful men because they don't feel they are *"in love"* any more. They don't hear any bells or whistles or see any stars. If you are a mature woman, you may be a bit taken aback by this. We know that the stars, whistles and bells only exist in the early stages of the relationship, if at all. But there are some women who refuse to allow the fairy tale to die. She wants her prince and she wants him to make her feel like a princess. Well, prince charming doesn't exist, except in fairy tales, and neither does the princess. We are suffering from romantic illusions. The wine and roses syndrome.

I was listening to a talk show, and heard a caller complaining about her boss. She had worked for him for a while. She was secretly in love with him, but had never told him (fantasy). Somehow he must have sensed it. He invited her out to dinner on a Friday evening. After dinner, they went back to his home for drinks. She ended up staying the weekend. She exclaimed, *"It was all so **romantic.**"* But, the romance didn't last long, because when she returned to work on Monday, it was business as usual. She could not understand how her boss could treat her that way. *"The sex was fantastic. It was like a **dream** come true."* For whom? For her evidently, but not for the boss. She went in under the illusion of romance, and her boss had his eyes wide open. She is fortunate she didn't come in to a pink slip.

This is so typical of women. Stars in their eyes. Fantasy comes true. Romance must mean he loves me, he cares about me. She didn't ask him. She just assumed if he romanced her, if he allowed her to spend the weekend at his home and had sex with her, he must want a permanent relationship with her. Imagine how she felt returning to work and having her boss act as if it had never happened. As women we need to cut out the romantic fantasy, and ask questions, before we jump into bed with a man. If we don't, we can't complain about being used . We can't blame him for our fantasy. Men tend not to get caught up in the romance trap the way women do. They understand it's part of a game.

In the early stages of the relationship, romance is dazzling. It sweeps you off your feet. Your head is spinning, your vision is blurred, and your hearing is impaired. You see only what you want to, and you hear only what you need to. A man reveals himself very early in a relationship. But, we are so busy playing Cinderella, or should I say Spinderella, that we miss the clues. By the time the smoke clears, we are so hooked, or so deep in you-know-what, we don't know truth from fantasy.

Anything he tells us we believe. I know women who stay in abusive relationships, because they fantasize about the romantic interludes they had with their abuser in the early stages of the relationship. You see, romance looks like, feels like, love. Some women fall into that trap. They keep hoping they will see that side again. They keep talking about how wonderful he was--in the beginning. They won't see that side again because it was never real. He's the same person he always was, but the smoke has cleared.

Some women spend their whole lives looking for the perfect relationship. If it doesn't look like, feel like, a certain thing (usually an image in her head) then he doesn't really love her. Actually, romance has nothing to do with love per se. Have you ever been romanced by a guy and once he got what he wanted, he was gone? Was that love? No, it was romance. It was an illusion. If his actions contradict what he says, pay close attention to the actions. They are the revealing factors.

As women, we so often fall into the romance trap. If he's bringing wine and roses, he must care. If he's taking me out to candlelight dinner, it must be love. If he cooks for me at his place, and runs me a bubble bath afterwards, he must be hearing wedding bells. Stop hallucinating. It could be that he has you figured out. I am not saying there is anything wrong with romance or a romantic evening. I am saying beware of the trap. Call it what it is. Romance is romance, and love can be something quite different, delightfully more exciting and definitely more lasting.

We are women of high achievement, pacesetters in the business world. We are in the major boardrooms of every major corporation in America. Not to mention the corporations we've set up on our own. We have conquered this career thing. Yet, many of us still live in the imaginary world of romance. Searching for love, but settling for romance, can become a habit. The danger is that when the smoke clears, there won't be anything left. Romance tricks you into believing that this is the way your life will always be. It's a myth. No one, including you, could possibly live up to that perfect illusion.

Whether you are ready or not, it's time to get on with real life. If it's love you are seeking, take a good, objective look at what it is you want. Love, real love, doesn't illuminate bigger than life when the candles are lit, only to go out when they are not. Real love casts a low, constant glow and illuminates over time- with care and devotion.

EXERCISE

Rather than fantasize about a prince charming that doesn't exist, write out a description of your Ideal Mate. (Be careful what you ask for; you might get it.) **My Ideal Mate:**

_____

_____

_____

_____

_____

_____

_____

_____

_____

List the qualities you bring to a relationship:

_____

_____

_____

_____

_____

_____

_____

_____

_____

_____

Self-Love Empowers Us

There was a song that said, it *takes a fool to learn that love don't love nobody.* What the song could have said is, *Love don't love nobody that doesn't love herself.* Love is incapable of loving a person that does not love herself. You must first love if you want to be loved. You must first love yourself if you want someone else to love you. God loved us first so that we could learn to love ourselves. He knows we are his greatest gift. But, somehow that love of self has gotten lost on us. I know we have all had to contend with this world, and we have had conflicting teachings about love. Some people believe it is selfish to love yourself first. But, I believe it is selfish to put the burden of responsibility on someone else to love you when you don't love yourself. It can become burdensome when you are trying to make someone else responsible for you, for your happiness, for making you feel good about yourself, for loving you. That is a big responsibility and most people eventually resent the burden or they simply refuse to accept it. If we go into a relationship trying to make the other person responsible for loving us, and we don't love ourselves, no matter how much they love us, we won't feel loved. We will always feel less than loved, and it will eventually show itself in our relationship. In the beginning we feel so good and so loved but, the burden becomes too great for our partners who are constantly trying to make us feel loved, and no matter how hard they try it doesn't work, because we don't love ourselves and it shows.

But when we love ourselves, when we have done the work , experienced the growth, accepted the challenge, created the new life, we have so much more to offer ourselves and the people who love us. We aren't going into relationships looking to be fixed. We aren't going into relationships trying to fix or change the other person. What we look for in and expect from relationship changes. Because we are different, our expectations are different.

No Problem Is Permanent

I was reading one of my favorite magazines *Ebony*, and I read a story that both hurt and shocked me. It could have been a real tragedy. It was an interview with a famous actress who was recently divorced. She talked about her tragic divorce, and then went on to talk about the thoughts of suicide she had entertained for several hours one night. She decided against it, and I am so thankful. She is beautiful, talented and successful, yet that is not enough. She still feels lacking in some way. I find that to be true with a lot of women. But, she did not take her life and we are still blessed with her presence.

No problem is permanent, as this actress has hopefully discovered by now. No problem effects every area of our lives. There is always something to be thankful for. Thoughts of suicide are thoughts of hopelessness. We are feeling defeated and depressed. No person, no disappointment, no loss is worth committing suicide. Life is always worth living. There is always something to be grateful for. When we are experiencing problems in one area of our lives that is the perfect time to concentrate on the other areas that are working. Concentrate on the good in your life. Concentrate on the blessings. If you can't find any in your own life, visit a mental hospital or an AIDS ward or a convalescent home. There are always people worse off than we are. These visits can sometimes help us to realize that our problems are not as bad as we thought. Remember, no problem is permanent. Every problem has a solution and nothing is ever final, except death as we know it.

EXERCISE

Even if your life looks terrible right now, there is always something to be thankful for. List as many good things as you can that you are thankful for. Examples: My health, my career, my spiritual beliefs, my talents, my relationship with my _____ (fill in the blank, for example with my best friend, my mother, etc..)

List as many as you can think of in all areas of your life. Do this anytime you feel depressed, sad or hopeless. We only feel these negative emotions because we are focusing on negative thoughts.. This exercise takes the focus away from what you don't have, and puts it on what you do have.

_____

_____

_____

_____

_____

_____

_____

_____

_____

_____

The "Need" To Feel Loved

This actress also said, she would find someone who is willing and able to *fill her love cup up.* Well, that cup may be real deep, and no one else may be capable of filling it up. I believe we need to fill it up ourselves first. It must be full of self-love. Then when another person comes into our lives, he will have no problem bringing his full cup to the party. But, suppose we get someone whose cup is empty too. Then nobody can fill anybody's cup up. I hate to see women take that kind of a chance. It can be emotionally devastating.

There was another statement that sparked some concern. She admitted to being *needy* and said that she was not ashamed of it. That's good she is not ashamed, but after the last experience I would not want to give anyone that kind of power over my life. So my suggestion would be to work on the neediness and the empty cup before getting into a new relationship. We can learn to be self-sufficient. We can learn to love ourselves enough so that a mate will be a blessing, not a crutch. The cup runneth over with love because it will already be full with self-love. Going into a relationship with an empty cup is a big gamble, and not many people win at gambling. I hope she has a good therapist. Because not all therapists believe in the same principles. I hope she has a therapist that can help her become responsible for her own love cup being filled and encourage her not to give that responsibility to another person .

I hope all women will eventually get the message that we alone are responsible for bringing a full cup to a relationship. No one can fill our love cup up, if we haven't filled it up with self-love. Believe me, I have been through it myself. There is probably not a woman out there that has not suffered that *"love and lost"* blues. I am not a martyr. I have worked hard over the last 15 years in the personal development field. I know how important it is to love yourself before you get into a relationship. One of the most important reasons is because we attract what we are, not what we want.

When we are too needy, we attract men who appear to be just what we *need*. Notice I said *appears* to be. Because they will be appealing to our neediness. Our need for validation. They may be incapable of meeting your emotional needs and may eventually resent you for it. But, we on the other hand, can learn to control our neediness, which is usually based on insecurities. Fear of being alone. Fear of not being able to take care of ourselves. Sometimes personal development can help but, if you have a deep emotional problem, you should seek a good therapist. But, understand that it is ok to ask for help. Are you full of fear and insecurities? Are you afraid of being alone? Do you have feelings of inadequacy? Do you feel incapable of dealing with it on your own? It is up to you to determine if you need professional help. If you determine you need it, get it. Don't feel you have to handle emotional problems alone.

I want to see women taking more responsibility for their relationships. Not being so emotional and dependent on their mates for their happiness. A relationship should be nourishing for both people. We need to take as much responsibility for our relationships as we do for our careers. Men are not equipped to fix us any more than we are equipped to fix them. We need to fix us and attract to us men who have done the work on themselves.

If you remember one thing remember this, we attract to us what we are, not what we want. So whatever you are and wherever you are in your relationship with yourself right now, it is important to know and recognize if there is still work to do. I am not suggesting that you not have male friends or that you not try again. I am suggesting you make sure you are ready for a romantic relationship and be totally realistic about what your expectations are, what your needs are, what you can handle.

So how do we get to this point in our lives? It takes continuous work. Each chapter in this book has an exercise at the end. Answering these questions will help you develop a Personal Development Plan as you proceed through the book. Take the time to answer the questions and write the answers down. Keep a journal or notebook by your side as you read. By the time you reach the end of this book, ¾ of the work will be completed. The other ¼ will be putting what you have learned into practice. I hope you are ready to make a commitment to new ways of acting, thinking, doing and being.

EXERCISE

Have you worked on yourself sufficiently?

Are you secure in yourself?

Have you really looked at and understood where your love barometer is these days? In other words, are you on full or empty?

Can you handle a disappointment right now?

Can you handle rejection?

Do you love yourself properly? (are you taking care of your own needs)?

Do you want a relationship to fill you up or to complement you?

If you simply read this book, or any book, and put it aside and do nothing, nothing will happen.   So I am including a commitment sheet .   I would like you to mail it back to me, stating you have read the book and you are doing the work. Do not destroy your book. Make a copy of this form and send it to me. Then send another copy 3 months from the date of the first note you sent me. Finally send me a copy of the second note 6 months after the date of the first note.   I will be looking forward to hearing from each of you. I know you can do it. It simply requires commitment and discipline. Both of which I am sure you have. May your blessings be plentiful.

Copy this form & send it to me after you read the book and again in 3 mos.

I _____on _____
　　　　　　　　　Name　　　　　　　　　　　　　　　　　Date

read the book *Loving Yourself First* and answered the questions.

I am doing the work.

_____
　　　　　　　　Signature

Send to:　　　Linda Coleman-Willis
　　　　　　　　P. O. Box 90369
　　　　　　　　Los Angeles, California 90009

Copy this form and send to me 6 months from date of first note:

I, _____ on _____
            Name   Date

have practiced the ideas, techniques and suggestions found in the book, *Loving Yourself First* for six months. I have / have not experienced significant changes in my life.

NOTE: If you failed to follow through for 3 months, try again. Keep trying until you can do it. If you can do it, you should see significant changes in your life.

_____
Signature

Send to: Linda Coleman-Willis
              P. O. Box 90369
              Los Angeles, California 90009

Chapter 3

Accept/Appreciate/Affirm Yourself

I was watching a television talk show, and a woman weighing about 500 pounds was one of the guests. The interview was telecast from her hospital room. She was so ill she could not leave the room. The show was about overweight people, but this particular story had another twist. She had a boyfriend whom she had given up her apartment, her child, her money, everything she owned for. And now she was homeless and broke, because he had lied and cheated and left her with nothing.

Her mother sat on the stage of the television show with her grandson, blaming the boyfriend for all her daughter's problems. As I watched and listened, I heard the classic case of "your cheating heart." No one mentioned what this woman was doing to herself and to her son. It was all about how this man not wanting her and using her had created all these problems in her life. The real issues were never dealt with. Her weight, her obvious lack of love for herself, her refusal to take responsibility, and her unhealthy need for and attachment to this man who obviously did not care about her. She loved him at the expense of herself and her child.

I remember thinking to myself, as I heard the host and the mother pound away at this guy for taking advantage of her while she was ill, even if this guy left her and never came back, she would have the same problems. Unless she is willing to handle all the other issues, and stop placing the blame elsewhere, on her mother, her boyfriend, her weight, she will continue to have the same challenges.

Ending The Blame Game

We make mistakes, then we spend the rest of our lives blaming something or someone else for our mistakes. We blame timing, the government, our circumstances, and our parents. We blame everyone but ourselves. If we can blame someone else, we don't have to look at ourselves.

As women, we so often do this. We look to put the blame elsewhere. Maybe someone else is to blame, but placing blame never made anything better. If we want things to change for the better, we have to accept responsibility and not play the blame game. If we get caught up in the blame game, we will not be able to get past whatever the problem really is. We will simply wallow in our misery, blaming someone else to ease our own conscience, but things will not get better until we stop blaming and start taking responsibility.

No man can make you happy, if you are unhappy with yourself. Trying to make men responsible for how we feel is self-defeating. That responsibility belongs to us. Everyone has the responsibility to make herself emotionally healthy, before they get involved with another person. If you believe a man can provide what you lack emotionally, you may be grossly disappointed. Stop looking for men to support you in ways you are not supporting yourself. Learn to care for yourself physically, financially and emotionally. When you do meet a man, he will enhance what you already are and what you already have.

It was interesting to me that no one ever said any of this to that woman. No one, not even her mother, told her that she bore some responsibility in this whole thing. That the guy they were all blaming was a symbol of a bigger problem she needed to deal with. Unless she gets some professional help, counseling from a qualified therapist, she is likely to repeat this scenario.

We have to learn to accept, appreciate and affirm ourselves. Accept yourself just as you are right now. It doesn't matter what you look like, what you do for a living, how much money you have, what kind of car you drive. None of that matters. You have to affirm that you are OK as you are, before you can hope to get better, to move forward. *"I love myself just as I am right now-mind, body and spirit."* Some people argue that if they love themselves just as they are, they may never change. Actually the reverse is true. If you can love yourself at your worst, it will be easy to love yourself at your best. In fact you must love yourself at your worst, if you ever hope to become your best. *"I accept myself totally, fully, wholly just as I am right now."*

You also have to affirm that you are who and what you are today because of the choices you have made in the past. It is very important that you take responsibility for the choices you have made, and not blame anyone else. *"I affirm that I am who I am right now because of the choices I made. Likewise, I will be who I am in the future because of the choices I will make." "I am committed to making better choices." "Therefore, I can become whatever I want to become based on what I am willing to do to get there."* This empowers you. The moment you take responsibility it gives you the power to change. It gives you the power to make better choices. You don't have to depend on someone else to make the decision for you. You can make it for yourself. Making better choices will improve your life.

Taking Personal Responsibility

In my opinion, this is one of the single most important words in the English language. **R E S P O N S I B I L I T Y.** Your ability to respond. Why? Because most of the problems we experience in life are because we fail to take responsibility. Look at your own life. Be honest with yourself. What problems can you identify that point back to your not taking responsibility, either in a timely fashion or not at all? I would be willing to bet about 90% or higher. We are a country of people who believe problems are always someone else's responsibility.

So you have a problem. And you have a good excuse for living with it, right?   You're unappreciated, misunderstood, your parents raised you wrong, the school didn't teach you the right thing, the system is against you, you're broke, unemployed, you can't do anything right, you made a lot of mistakes when you were young. There is nothing you can do about it because you are too old, too young, too tall or too short. You are under-educated, overweight, you won't conform, and you don't have any money.

Do you realize these are all excuses? When we don't want to do something, or don't want to take responsibility for something, we can always find an excuse that will let us off the hook.   We quite often look to other people to solve our problems for us. Now let's face reality. People are just more concerned about their own problems than they are about yours. And you can't change them. This means that you, and you alone, must take responsibility for solving your problems and living your own life.

Being responsible requires that we make decisions. And making decisions require that we be responsible for the outcome, good or bad. Now that's ok if the outcome is good, but what happens when the outcome is bad? That's right. We start looking around for someone else to blame. Look back on your own life. Accept your mistakes, take full responsibility for them. Stop making excuses for your mistakes. **(Repeat After Me)** *"I am responsible for my life."* *"I am responsible for my dreams."*   Your life is in the best hands it could possibly be in, your own. I have a question for you, *"Whose life is it anyway?"* Besides no one else is going to take the responsibility, even if you wanted him to. People are good at telling us what we can't do, but we usually have to remind ourselves what we can do.

My suggestion to you is: **Take responsibility for whatever you want to have happen in your own life.** I used to think all I had to do was be good at something, and sooner or later someone would notice, and would come up to me and say, *"You are so good I want to make you a star or make you rich."* It could happen that way, but the chances of that ever happening are probably about a million to one. No matter how good I was, nothing happened until I took the initiative to make it happen. When I started taking responsibility for what I wanted, my life changed.

If you want something to happen, take the responsibility for making it happen. If you need help, ask for it. Les Brown always says you have to *"A S K to G E T."* So if you are a person who has never been good at taking responsibility, look around and find the most responsible person you know and ask for help. You can also take on small projects and see them through to completion. Then slowly increase the amount of responsibility you take on. The more we do, the more we can do, and the better we get.

Accept 100% responsibility for what happens in your life, and know that you have the power to take control of many aspects of your life, mental and physical. Self-control is the key. Take responsibility for creating, developing, and maintaining your place in this world. It's not so much what happens to you in life, but how you handle it. How you respond to it. Whether or not you are willing to step up to the plate and be responsible. Be sure to answer the questions at the end of this chapter on responsibility.   They will help you understand your beliefs about responsibility, and to become more responsible.

Answer the following questions:

What are we responsible for? When is it absolutely necessary for us to take responsibility or is it ever absolutely necessary for us to take responsibility? What happens to us when we allow someone or something else to become responsible for us? Do we give up something? Are you willing to take that kind of chance with your life?

1. Most people do not accept personal responsibility for what they are and where they are. They tend to blame others, circumstances, and things. Why do you suppose this is?

2. What responsibilities do you have as a member of a family? As a member of a group? To your community?

3. What have you been avoiding taking responsibility for? Why? Are you better prepared now to take responsibility? (Whatever the answer to this question start now to take responsibility for it. Do something small, then build up to something bigger until you have handled it.)

Changing Habits

You are what you are based on habits, and you will be in the future where your habits lead you. Everything we do becomes a habit if we do it long enough. Lots of things we do are bad habits. Why do we continue these habits long after they have stopped serving our needs? Because they are comfortable, familiar and easy. Going outside our comfort level requires that we change, stretch and grow. We are perfectly happy and content with the familiar, the tried and the true. Change requires us to change a habit or several habits. Changing habits are difficult and require a great amount of effort. Then, there is the fear of not being able to change, of feeling like a failure. But, you can change your bad habits, and you can change for the better. You just have to know what to do, and be willing to do it. Identify the habits that are not serving your needs anymore, that are not getting you what you want, that are not taking you where you want to go. Make a commitment to change them. The exercise at the end of the chapter will help you identify the habits you want to change.

You must take responsibility for changing whatever it is you know you need to change. Reaffirm yourself every step of the way. The important thing to remember is we have to accept, appreciate and affirm ourselves right where we are. I hear so many women putting themselves down. They say to themselves "I hate my _____ " (you fill in the blank). Whatever it is you hate, it is much harder to change while hating yourself than it is while loving yourself. Let's say your problem is you are overweight, and the things you hate are your fat thighs. If it's the fat thighs you hate, affirm them. Now touch them and say, "F*at thighs, I love you just the way* you are." Use affirmations and visualization (see exercise at the end of chapter one for definitions). Close your eyes and see your thighs becoming smaller. Talk to those fat thighs. *"You have been with me a long time. I have needed you to assist me in getting around. You did that and I appreciate you. I love you. Now you and I working together can reduce the amount of fat, because we both need to be slimmer so we can accomplish our new goals together." "I need you, I love you and I appreciate you."* Do the same for your stomach, arms, and any other parts of your body you find yourself not appreciating or being ashamed of. Remember these body parts have served you all your life. It is the choices you made that put them in the condition they are in now. You need to reaffirm this and make it OK that they are the way they are right now but, begin working to make them the way you want them to be. This empowers you. It takes the shame and guilt away. It makes it OK to be less than perfect. It makes it OK to be who and what you are right now. This opens up the way for you to become who and what you want to be in the future. It's very difficult to lose weight, hating who you are or any part of you. Hate is a negative emotion and produces negative results. If you accept, appreciate and affirm yourself, you can love yourself wherever you find yourself. This empowers you to change.

EXERCISE

Identify the habits that are not getting you what you want, and make a commitment to change them. Write them down in the table below. For every habit you want to change, list a new habit to take its place. Select one new habit and make a commitment to practice it for 30-days. By the end of the thirty-days, you should have a new habit. Then select another one until you have completed your list. If at first you don't succeed, try again and keep trying until you have all new habits.

Habits I Want to Change   **Replacement Habits**

_____   _____

_____   _____

_____   _____

_____   _____

_____   _____

_____   _____

_____   _____

_____   _____

_____   _____

_____   _____

_____   _____

_____   _____

_____   _____

Chapter 4

The Keys To Successful Living

R-E-S-P-E-C-T Yourself

If you don't, no one else will. We can learn to respect ourselves. Lack of respect is one of the biggest problems we face. Lack of respect for ourselves and for other people. If you want respect, you must give respect. We cannot expect other people to respect us if we don't respect ourselves. When we subject ourselves to things that we don't want in our lives, because of peer pressure or because we want someone to like us or accept us, we are not respecting ourselves and we will ultimately lose the respect of the very people we are trying to impress. When we respect ourselves, we only allow good positive experiences into our lives. When we respect ourselves we do not participate in activities, thoughts or ideas that do not coincide with what we want. Respect wins friends and influences people. Respect for ourselves and for other people paves the way for more success, happiness and satisfaction to come into our lives. When we are disrespectful of ourselves, our bodies, our relationships, our time, we lose. We lose our health, our money, our loved ones, everything valuable. Respect is easy when you know what it is that you value. If you value and respect life you will not take foolish chances.

I see mothers do all kinds of things in front of their children and say anything to their children. Then they wonder why their children have no respect for them. We have to earn the respect of our children. It doesn't come automatically. We earn respect by giving it. I know this sounds elementary, but based on some of the stories I have shared with you in this book, and some of the things I have seen, it is not automatic. Young children are allowed to watch any type of movie and listen to any type of music and when they have an attitude the parent is upset. They are mimicking what they hear and see. Unfortunately children don't do what you say, they do what they see you do. Not only do they lose respect for you, they don't have any respect for themselves. When they don't respect themselves, they don't respect anyone else. Respect is very important because it leads to self-love which is what this book is all about.

It seems today that no one has any respect for anyone else. That is a sad statement. I host a weekly radio talk show in Los Angeles *The Motivation Power Hour*. I remember doing a show on *"Anger Management"*. My guest was an accomplished psychologist, Dr. Floyd McGregor. About a half-hour into the show, we got a call from an elderly gentleman. He lived near a high school. He was very angry and complained about how rude and disrespectful the high-school children were. He started out complaining vigorously about how terrible they were. He kept saying over and over *"I'm so angry."* After several minutes of dialogue back and forth with Dr. McGregor, he finally admitted, in tears, that all he wanted from the young people was a little respect. They did not know his story, his life, or his history. They discounted him simply because he was old. They made fun of him and disrespected him, yet he said he really wanted to help them, to share with them, to be a role model for them. But, all he got from them was taunting and teasing. In the end he would have settled for a little respect. It made me very sad to hear this elderly gentleman break down and cry on my show. He sobbed over and over, *"They have no respect."*

Why is it that our young people have no respect for the elderly? Could it be they are taking their cues from us? What happened? Why is it we are not demanding respect? Is it because we are not giving it that we are not getting it? Why are we not at least teaching our children to respect the elderly?

Is respect old fashioned and outdated? Can we expect to have healthy relationships, harmonious communities, productive societies and children who respect us when we are elderly if we neglect to teach them how?

Can we turn the tide? You bet we can. Starting with each one of us. Practice respect with your children, your spouse, your parents, and your neighbors using three little phases: thank you, excuse me and please. Be respectful to strangers on the street and oh yeah—which is what this section is all about—be respectful to yourself. It feels really good to give and receive respect because you will have earned it.

EXERCISE

Do I respect the rights of others?
Am I deserving of other's respect?
How do I demonstrate respect for myself? For other people?
Am I teaching my children to respect themselves? To respect others?
Do I have a relationship with an elderly person? Am I willing to develop one?

Developing High Self-Esteem

What is self-esteem? Self-esteem is self-confidence, self-worth and self-respect. It is appreciating one's own worth and importance, and respecting the worth and value of others.

Self-esteem is a state of mind. It is the way you feel and think about yourself and others; and it is measured by the way you act. Your self-esteem serves as the bridge between who you are and what you do. It can be defined as your internal belief system as well as how you experience life externally.

Each of us is born with the capacity for positive feelings, but it is possible to learn to not like yourself through practice and/or through life experiences. There are many reasons for low self-esteem. Childhood experiences, criticism from adults and/or peers, your environment, cultural background, negative images from society in general. If these negative feelings are reinforced by your own beliefs, low self-esteem can become the norm for your life. When we adopt negative images of ourselves as true, whether they are true or not, they effect our self-esteem. Unfortunately, too many people feel bad about themselves. They are overly critical of themselves, and accept too readily the opinion of others about who they are.

Self-esteem changes, depending on what you experience or how you are feeling. If you want to be happy and successful personally and professionally, you have to feel good about yourself. Self-esteem effects everything we do, think or say. It effects how we live our lives, conduct our relationships and the choices we make. People who feel good about themselves produce positive results.

The key to elevated self-esteem is the willingness to take responsibility for your feelings, desires, thoughts, abilities and interests and to accept your overall strengths and act accordingly.

In order to maintain high self-esteem, we must believe in ourselves and in our self-worth. Be able to see our place in the world realistically and optimistically. Have confidence in our abilities to meet life's challenges. We must have a knowledge and acceptance of self. The ability to recognize our individual uniqueness and take pride in that uniqueness. The confidence to try something new. Understand that we have value, regardless of the situation or any specific performance. Love ourselves enough to take the responsibility for designing and creating our lives the way we want them to be.

As a speaker traveling across the country and meeting lots of people, I get letters all the time from women who don't feel good about themselves for one reason or another. A great deal of these women has their careers together, but their personal lives are in shambles. Nine times out of ten it is in shambles because of a failed relationship. I received a letter from a woman that went something like this: *I am in a rut, lost, don't know my life's purpose, don't know what I want as a career, low self-esteem... Since my husband left our two children and me I seem to be trapped in this rut, not able to accept the divorce and just standing still in life. Everything seems to have gone down hill. I hope your tape program "How To Change Your Life" can bring me out of this darkness and awaken me to life again...*

One of the saddest things about this letter was her husband left her 15 years ago. But, she wrote as if it were yesterday. She is stuck in the past and has not gotten beyond the hurt and pain of her divorce. It hurts my heart when I receive letters like this one because I know the possibilities for her life. But, it is she who has to recognize them. She will never recognize them being stuck in the past. It is time wasted that can never be replaced. When we spend our life living in the past, time passes us by. What about the two children? This cannot be good for them. I can only pray that something she hears on my tape, or someone or something else, comes along and wakes her up. Fifteen years is long enough. The only place the past can exist is in our minds, memories and thoughts. You cannot heal or grow, living in the past. Get over past hurts by:

1. Releasing them.
2. Living in the present.
3. Planning the future.
4. Facing and dealing with the pain.

We have to be willing to let go.   Repeat the following affirmations at least three times a day.   Record these affirmations in your own voice and listen to them every chance you get.   Total relaxation is the ideal situation.   Hold each affirmation in your mind for at least 30 seconds.   Don't give up after a few tries.   If you continue, you will notice a change, first in the way you feel, then in the things you do and say.   Your life will change for the better.

I release all past hurts, failures and disappointments.
I am free of any personal limitation, lack, doubt, or inferiority.   I am entering a new level of understanding and consciousness of a richer, more meaningful life.   I am vitalized by new ambitions, dreams and excitement for living.

Self-awareness is the first step to change.   Be aware of how you feel about yourself.   Know that decisions you made about yourself when you were young need to be re-evaluated.   Focus your energy on letting go of unwarranted negative images, and replacing them with positive ones.   No one else will ever be you.   You are unique and you are special.   One of a kind. Appreciate and accept your good points and love yourself in spite of your bad ones.   We all have them.   Don't stay around negative people.   People who put you or themselves down. Don't spend time worrying about what other people think about you.   Eleanor Roosevelt said: *"You wouldn't worry so much about what other people thought if you realized how seldom they do."*   She also said: *"No one can make you feel inferior without your consent."*

Exercises To Increase Self Esteem

1. Make an "I Am Unique List." Write down all the things that are unique about you (ask friends how they see your uniqueness.)

2. List 5 things that you do very well.

3. Make a pride list (things that you are proud of.)

4. Write five positive words that describe you.

5. Feed your mind and your Ego will be fed: Read books and listen to tapes that inspire and motivate, take classes, go to seminars and lectures, take up hobbies, surround yourself with positive people. (Never use artificial stimulants such as drugs or alcohol. The changes don't last, and the results can be devastating.)

6. List five negative messages you remember hearing as a child or that you still hear today. Take these negative statements and turn them into positive ones. (Use I or My in the present tense.) Example: If someone calls you stupid, your turnaround statement could be *"I am an intelligent person."* If you were told you would never amount to anything, your turnaround statement could be *"I am very successful in everything that I do."*

7. REMEMBER, GOD DIDN'T MAKE ANY JUNK! Use affirmations to remind yourself how wonderful you are. Feeling good about you is not a luxury; it is an absolute necessity. *"Day by day in every way I am*

getting better and better." " I am a unique, confident interesting human being."

10 Keys To Developing Self Esteem In Children

The National Institute of Mental Health asked 50 parents, who had raised their children to become well-adjusted, productive adults the following question:

Based on your personal experiences, "What are the best advice you can give to new parents about raising children?" Following is a summary of their responses:

1. LOVE ABUNDANTLY. The most important task is to love and really care about your child. This gives him or her a sense of security, belonging and support. It smoothes the rough edges of society.

2. DISCIPLINE CONSTRUCTIVELY. Give clear direction and enforce the limits on your child's behavior. Emphasize **"Do this,"** instead of **"Don't do that."**

3. WHENEVER POSSIBLE, SPEND TIME WITH YOUR CHILDREN. Play with them, talk to them, teach them to develop a family spirit and give them a sense of belonging.

4. GIVE THE NEEDS OF YOUR MATE PRIORITY. A husband and wife are more likely to be successful parents when they put their marriage first. Don't worry

about the children getting "second best." Child-centered households do not produce happy marriages or happy children.

5. TEACH YOUR CHILDREN RIGHT FROM WRONG. They need to be taught basic values and manners so they will get along well in society. Insist that they treat others with kindness, respect and honesty. Set personal examples of moral courage and integrity.

6. DEVELOP MUTUAL RESPECT. Act in a respectful way toward your children. Say "please" and "thank you," and apologize when you are wrong. Children who are treated with respect will then know how to treat others respectfully.

7. LISTEN, REALLY LISTEN. This means giving your children undivided attention, putting aside your beliefs and feelings and trying to understand your children's point of view.

8. OFFER GUIDANCE. Be brief. Don't give speeches. And don't force your opinions on your children.

9. FOSTER INDEPENDENCE. Gradually allow children more freedom and control over their lives. One parent said, "Once your children are old enough, phase yourself out of the picture, but always be near when they need you."

10. BE REALISTIC, EXPECT TO MAKE MISTAKES. Be aware that outside influences such as peer pressure

will increase as children mature. Don't expect things to go well all the time. Child rearing has never been easy. It has its sorrows and heartaches, but it also has rewards and joys.

Valuing Yourself

What do you see when you look at someone who is very successful? You should be able to see at least that much and more when you look at yourself. Why is it we can see it in other people and we can't see it in ourselves? What makes it possible for others and impossible for us? Why not pretend to see yourself in the same light you see your favorite movie star or singer or dancer or anyone else you hold in esteem? Why not look at yourself through the same eyes? Oh, it's because you have not achieved the same level of success. To that I say sooo what? It doesn't matter. If you can began to look at yourself in the same light, hold your self in high esteem and visualize yourself as being as important as they are, it can happen. We must be willing to at least value our lives and ourselves as much as we value the lives of others. If we see an actress, we think her existence is so much more important than our own, because she has the good fortune to be living her dream. As long as we shower that importance on others, and we do not save any for ourselves, we will always be worshipping other people's successes and devaluing our own. It's ok to admire and respect what another person has accomplished, but it is not ok to worship others at the expense of hating ourselves because we have not accomplished or achieved our dreams. It is not ok to elevate their importance while diminishing our own.

I will never forget the evening my sister, a very successful attorney, and I went to an event held in Los Angeles called "A Mid-Summer Night's Magic." It was a dinner and all-star celebrity basketball game hosted by Earvin "Magic" Johnson. My sister and I had been invited to a VIP reception held prior to the game. We were both on the Board of Directors for The United Negro College Fund (UNCF). This was the recipient organization of the proceeds from Mid-Summer Night's Magic. What transpired that evening I will never forget. It significantly changed my life. Magic Johnson was standing in a dugout-type forum waiting to greet the guests. People were lining up to shake his hand. There were approximately 20 people in line (men, women and children) when my sister and I got in the line. We had been standing in the line about 5 minutes when the Public Relations person (who shall remain nameless) walked up to us and said "Sorry, this line is for VIP's only. You are in the wrong line." I was shocked and pissed off, but we left the line. This lady did not know who we were. She made assumptions based on what? Was it something we did or did not do? I do not know how my sister felt as we left the "VIP" line, but I was hurt, embarrassed and angry. The nerve of this woman. I was angry that she did not realize that I was a "VIP," and I was angry with myself for getting out of the line. I blamed her for my feelings of inadequacy. I promised myself that day that no one would ever make me feel that way again. I'll show her, I'll go out and become a VIP. A somebody. A success.

What I didn't realize at that time was, I am already a VIP, a somebody, a success. She could not make me feel inadequate unless I already felt that way. It was not her fault how I felt about what she did. It wasn't what she thought of me that made me get out of that line it was what I thought of myself. It would not have mattered what she said to me if I had thought of myself as a VIP. Obviously I didn't think I was a Very Important Person. I got out of the line and I felt about as small as an ant. She didn't recognize it because I didn't recognize it. If I had I would have told her *"VIP, that means I'm in the right line."*

Other people cannot tell you what to think or how to feel about yourself. Only you can do that. We cannot control other people, but we can control how we think and therefore how we act, what we do or choose not to do. We are in control and we must value ourselves as important human beings. I wasn't loving myself first, I was loving Magic Johnson first. I wasn't valuing me; I was valuing him. I am not saying he is not valuable, but so am I. The moment I began to acknowledge my own value as a human being, my life began to change.

I want you to stop reading right now and go to the end of this chapter and write down the things about you that you value most. Be careful that they are not all-physical things. It's OK that we love our hair, looks or other physical characteristics, but look beyond the physical. Also take a look at the things in your life that you value the most. Be careful that they are not all-material possessions. If they are, forget about the material possessions for now, and look at the other things that are important in your life. Get in the habit of keeping a journal. Write in it often the things that make you both happy and sad. Write down the things you do well and the things you would like to improve. Write down how you feel on a daily basis. Write down your disappointments as well as your successes.

When you go back months or even years later, you will be surprised how much you have grown. You will be able to see your life as it was and as it is now. A very interesting experience.

Do not allow other people to determine how you feel about you. We are all VIP's so we should all act and treat ourselves like VIP's. If other people fail to recognize it, that is their problem. As long as you recognize it you will not allow yourself to be treated any other way.

EXERCISE

Write down the things about yourself that you value.   Be
careful that they are not all-physical things.   It's OK that we
love our hair, looks or other physical characteristics but, look
beyond the physical.

What is it about your personality?

vivacious _kind_

bubbly _warm_

sparkle

loving

sweet

joyful

Your mind?

smart _great sens of humor_

brilliant

super-creative

imaginative

Your abilities?

strong

resourceful

intuitive

caring

loving

Your talents?

- great w/ public
connecting
nurturing
uplifting
loving
lightening up

Your accomplishments?

• published author
• great mother
• good writer
• excellent on TV
• great interview
• great partner

Also take a look at the things in your life that you value the most. Be careful that they are not all-material possessions. If they are, forget about the material possessions for now and look at the other things that are important in your life. **Family, Friendships, Relationships, Health, Spirituality, Beliefs, Hobbies, Goals, etc.**

Get in the habit of keeping a journal. Write in it often the things that make you both happy and sad. Write down the things you do well and the things you would like to improve. Write down how you feel on a daily basis. Write down your disappointments as well as your successes.

Valuing The Children

Let's talk about valuing our children and teaching them to value themselves. I could not write a book about loving yourself first without addressing this very important part of our lives. Our most valuable assets in the whole world are our children. Steven Covey says in his book *The 7 Habits of Highly Effective People, that we can be "transitional people." "There are only two lasting bequests we can give our children—one is roots, the other wings."* We can give them wings to fly. They don't have to be stuck with all the old garbage we were stuck with.

Transitional means change. We can change the way our children think about life, about themselves, about their history and about their future. We don't have to burden them with the things we were burdened with. We can change all that. We can be transitional people. We can change the next generation to come by leaving them a different legacy. Our generation has that kind of power. We can teach our children whatever we want them to learn. We can teach them how valuable they are. We can teach them about the power they possess and their innate ability to control and direct their own lives. They don't have to be stuck with the burdens of their past. We want to teach them their past only as a stepping stone to their future, not as a burden to bear.

As parents we are the first teachers. We have an opportunity that no one else has. That opportunity is to teach our children to love themselves unconditionally. I mean truly value who they are, not because they are wearing a $150 pair of tennis shoes, but because of whom they are inside. Buying expensive clothing to dress up the outside does no good, if we are not providing quality information to the inside, and teaching them to value themselves more than the tennis shoes. We are sending the wrong message. Expensive tennis shoes are not the answer. Expensive clothing is not the answer. We have to look beyond all that to the human being. We have to teach our children to look beyond the outer appearance, to value who they are and the power they possess. Personal power cannot be bought unless you are buying a book, or tape or seminar or an educational class. But, it does not come in a shoebox. Because you put on a pair of name-brand tennis shoes, you are not going to transform into some super-star athlete. Our children are buying into this. Heck, we appear to have bought into it ourselves. But, we have to teach them better.

Explain how a person becomes successful. It doesn't matter whether it's on the basketball court, in a classroom, or courtroom. You have to study hard, work hard, get an education and then you can compete. You have to be committed, persistent, and resilient. We have to teach them how to keep trying after failure. To stay in the chase for the long haul. They need to understand that success takes time and doesn't come easy. But, we can teach them to enjoy the journey and appreciate their efforts.

We must start now teaching our children to value themselves more than they value material possessions. And we do that by valuing ourselves more than material possessions. We do that by recognizing our children as our most valuable assets and treating them accordingly. We cannot continue to treat our cars and homes better than we treat our children. We cannot continue to spend more time developing a career than we spend developing our children. Our children are an investment in our future and the future of the world. We have to know that we are creating our own future through our children. If they are misguided, what kind of future will they have? What kind of future will we have? We are all in this together. We have to work together to make sure children know they are valuable and valued. We have to make sure our children know that there is hope for their future. That they can control their future by controlling what they do today, tomorrow and next week. They must know that if they do not like what they see, they have the power to change it.

Working with children ages 12-17 over the past few years has taught me a lot. Many of the children today don't believe they have the power to change things, to direct and control their own lives, to make a difference in the world. They are not sure if they can make a difference in their own lives. We have to instill hope for a better tomorrow in our children. Teach them how to dream. Make it ok for them to have dreams. Provide them with love, support and direction so they can achieve those dreams.

As parents it is our responsibility to teach and show our children that most of the stuff they see on television is not reality. If they are going to get $150 tennis shoes they have to earn them, need them, and not get them at the expense of something else that is needed more. As a matter of fact, a better lesson would be to teach them to take the $150 and invest in tennis-shoe stock rather than in the shoe itself. After all the return on the investment would be much greater (that's what Oprah Winfrey did). You see long after the tennis shoes are gone, the children would still have something of value, the stock. Chances are, the stock will be worth more than they paid for it. If we teach our children the real value of money, and the value of saving and investing money, they will benefit so much more than if we gave them expensive gifts. (There are reference books listed in the back of this book that deal with investments). Children are never too young to learn. Did anyone teach you? Chances are the answer is NO. So why not give your child a better start down the saving/investing road than you got? If all they do is spend, spend, spend their lives will be no better, maybe even worse, than ours. Let's give them a new legacy, a new beginning free of debt and free of poverty thinking. Encourage them to become savers, investors and entrepreneurs.

Education is the other important legacy we have to give our children. Education has to be more important than looking good. That means a book or class or homework or study time has to be more important than making sure your kids have expensive clothes and shoes. Reading classes should be more important than the latest toy. It's ok to give our kids some things, but it is more important that they earn the more expensive ones. The earlier they learn there is a price to pay for things, that nothing comes without some responsibility, the better off they will be. They will learn to value their possessions and to value hard work. But, the most important lesson we can teach our children is to value themselves. Get help if you need to. There are family counselors, therapists, spiritual leaders and teachers that will gladly help you teach your child values. There are books written on the subject. This may appear to be an uphill battle, but it has to begin with us, as parents. We have the most influence on our children in the earlier years of their lives. This is when we can make the biggest difference. The most valuable assets we have are our children. The time and energy spent will be well worth it.

EXERCISE

Write down the values that you want to teach your children. Values such as honesty, work ethics, being responsible, study habits, caring & compassion, fairness, etc. Pick one and concentrate on teaching that one for the entire month. Reward them at the end of the month. Then select another one, and so forth, until you have taught your children the values you want them to have. Make it a game and make it fun. If you go to a bookstore, especially a spiritual bookstore, you can find games and books dealing with teaching children values. These books will be a great addition to your library. (It takes time and energy, but don't you believe your children are worth it?)

Take your children to a bank and let them see how to set up a savings account. Then give them a bank and help them save money. It doesn't matter how much they save, as long as they save on a consistent basis. If they get a dime, have them put a nickel in the bank at home and spend the other nickel. If it's a dollar have them put 25cents or 50 cents in the bank and spend the rest. It's the habit of saving that we are trying to create. When the bank is full, take them to the real bank and deposit the money in a savings account. Don't go back and get it, unless they are ready to use it for a profit-making venture or an investment. You will be helping your children develop an attitude about money that can benefit them the rest of their lives. This is a better gift than leaving them large sums of money without the skills to handle it. Remember the old saying: *You give a child a fish you feed her for a day. Teach her how to fish, you feed her for life.*

Chapter 5

Linda Speaks...On Being A Single Mother

I remember being with women at work who talked about motherhood as if it were the most wonderful experience on earth. At the time I was a single mom, and I did not share their joy. I loved my children more than life itself, but I was not enjoying motherhood. I used to listen to them and wonder how they would fare as single parents. What kind of stories would they tell, if for some reason they were suddenly bread winner, head cook and housekeeper, and they still had to give love, guidance and direction to their children? How much of that joy for motherhood would they have? I would like to have felt as they felt. But, I didn't have the life they had. It was a struggle just to be there and be there on time everyday.

Those of you who are single moms, I commend you because I know it is not easy. Especially while you are in the throes of raising your children. No one seems to quite understand what you are going through. For the most part, people seem to be quick to judge, quick to give unsolicited advice, quick to point out what you should have done, could have done, or what they would have done, but seldom do they provide any real support. Not only does everyone expect you to be a martyr, but also they expect you to be everywhere at the same time, doing everything for everybody. Believe me I know; I have been there.

The best news I can give you as a single mom who has hung in there, raised your kids, paid the bills, kept yourself and the household together, maintained your sanity, loved your children, instilled values, cleaned wounds, baked cookies, went to club meetings, fixed broken toys and body parts, done homework, cleaned house, combed hair, patched & ironed clothes, cooked meals, read bedtime stories, colored pictures, joined dots, said prayers, washed faces, and cleaned fingerprints from the wall, gum from the carpet, cereal from the floor, and crumbs from the table, broken up fights, been the hero and the villain, the best friend and the worst enemy, stayed up late waiting, wondering, and worrying, sleepless nights, hospital visits in the middle of the night--is that you have developed one of the most important life skills, it's called *survival*. You came through wounded, but it wasn't fatal. You are a stronger, better person than when you began. Congratulations! You are now qualified for a lifetime membership in *The Wounded, But Not Fatal, Survivor's Club*. Here is your certificate of honor.

Certificate of Honor

The Wounded, But Not Fatal, Survivor's Club

Lifetime Membership

I remember the challenges of being a single mother. Always putting the kids, job, and the relationship first. Making sacrifices not everyone has to make or not willing to make. It wasn't so bad that we sacrificed so much; it was that no one ever seemed to notice. I guess we made it look too easy. We did such an outstanding job of hiding our feelings, doubts, fears, and our own needs, that no one but us and God knew the truth. Ohhh, I remember those late-night talks with God. I don't know if I could have made it through those times as a single parent, if those late night prayers had not been answered. Thank you, God!

We dared not tell anyone how many nights we lay in bed unable to sleep. Doubt, fear and uncertainty our constant companions. Never knowing if we were making the right decision or doing the right thing. I didn't do everything right, but I stayed. I remember, when things were exceptionally hectic, my thoughts of getting in the car and driving until I ended up who knew where. Maybe I would just disappear off the face of the earth. Anyway, they were just thoughts. I bet you thought you were the only person who felt that way. I believe most single parents have felt that way at one time or another. Fortunately, most of us only think about it; we would never actually do it. It's a form of escape, and it has probably helped reduce lots of stress for some very weary women.

Being a single parent, with all the challenges we face, seems to have very different outcomes for the parent and the children. It seems to make a mother stronger if she stays and handles it. If she hangs in there with her children, she becomes wise beyond her years. She gains insight and knowledge she wouldn't find in school or college. She learns first-hand what it takes to be successful in life. What it takes to survive and thrive. She knows how to overcome obstacles and challenges. How to make something out of nothing. She created the term "Give me a break."

What About The Children?

The children don't seem to fare as well, for the most part. True, a large number of them go on to college and get good jobs or careers, the gauges that society sets to determine whether or not we are successful. But, no one looks at their emotional lives to measure success. I am discussing women here, because the book is for and about women. I raised two women. I also worked with, knew, heard about, observed and talked to lots of women who were raised in a single-parent household.

The female child seems to be trying to find a father figure to replace the one that was never there. She seems to have a constant fear of being abandoned. Therefore, she tends to make poor choices in men. She doesn't seem to understand why her relationships don't work. She makes her selections based on men she believes need her, therefore they will always be there. And they are--in the beginning.

It doesn't matter how successful she becomes by society's standards. That feeling is there deep down inside of her and it doesn't just go away. She has to acknowledge it, and then there is work to do. She may not recognize it herself, therefore may deny its existence. I am not a psychologist or a psychiatrist, so I am only making observations; and speaking from my own personal experience and my experience as a trainer/facilitator in several programs, including a drug education program, teen-pregnancy program, juvenile-delinquency program, and several educational programs for high-school seniors and kids at risk.

You may choose to ignore the previous statements and write them off as my personal gripe session, but I felt they needed to be mentioned. There are too many of us out there. We need an organization—*"Single Parents of America and of the World."* We have survived. Our children have survived. We should at least be there for each other. I am not bitter. It was my decision to have children before I was prepared. I was married and thought we would raise them together, but it did not happen. My saddest moments are not about my struggle, but how our children suffered in a divorce situation. How the parent and children sometimes suffer in a single-parent household. That suffering is compounded if the parent left to care for the child is young, inexperienced, and has little or no parenting skills.

That is evidenced by how I hear some parents talk to their children. They will say anything to their child. I have heard parents in public places calling children every kind of four-letter word you can imagine. Also calling them words like *"stupid," "ignorant," "bad,"* and so on. If we, as parents, call our own children by these names, what kind of self-image will they have? How can they love and respect themselves, you, or anyone else, if their images of themselves are tied to these negative descriptions? I provide self-esteem and attitude seminars for several programs. Some of the children have come to me afterwards and said their parents put them down all the time. Their parents tell them their dreams are stupid. That they will never amount to anything. If you feel that way, keep it to yourself. I know that sometimes parents tell children what they think is a safe path to take in life. They love their children and don't want them to get hurt or to fail. But, you do not have the right to kill off your child's dream. You don't know what your child is capable of. You don't know what elements may come into play to help that child achieve her dream. If you can't see it for her, that is ok, don't discourage her. Try to support her anyway. Dreams are achieved because someone believed in a dream strong enough and long enough, until they convinced someone else to believe in it that had the ability to help make it come true. No one succeeds by herself. There are always other people who helped. You don't know who may be willing to help your child. If you can't help her, please don't hurt her, by squashing her dreams. Listen to her ideas, no matter how far-fetched they may be. There are lots of success stories out there whose original idea seemed far-fetched. We are living in a world and a time in history where almost anything is possible. If we can see it, we can be it. If we can believe it, we can achieve it. If we are willing to work for it, it is almost guaranteed that we will get it. That is the message we need to give our children. That is the message I try to instill in my students.

We have to hold ourselves in check with our children. There are few, if any, laws to protect children from emotional abuse. However, the scars are just as deep and the hurt just as lasting as with physical abuse. The spirit and the psyche are damaged, and the child grows up with self-hatred that translates into hate and destruction for the people around them.

One of the biggest problems with divorce is that the parents are usually licking their own wounds and don't realize how the children are affected, or don't know what to do about it. The children **are** affected and they need help getting through it, just as the adults do. They often appear to be handling it, but most kids are not prepared to handle it. Think about you, how well did you handle it? Multiply that by at least ten and that should tell you something about how your children are handling it. Get a family therapist. You and the kids can go together. Make sure it is a **family** therapist. Get a referral from someone you trust. Your doctor, a teacher, school counselor or your church. Talk to the counselor to make sure they share your values.

Prayer always worked for me. Get some good kneepads, because you will be on your knees a lot. Especially if you have teenagers. Start a support group if there are none in your community. Contact Family Services in your City or County or your school's counselor for a referral. Your spiritual leader should be able to help. The church is an excellent extended family as long as it is progressive, supportive, and has family-oriented programs in place. Despite what the media tries to portray, you **can** raise kids that are happy, healthy and well adjusted.

What's Age Got To Do With It?

Single moms, please don't condemn yourselves. There are lots of reasons for these problems. It is not just the fact that you are a single and/or divorced mom. Let me share with you another experience I had. I worked with a teen-pregnancy program, where the youngest girl in the group was 13. Her mother was 28. The average age of the girls was 15–16. The average age of the parents was 30–36. Ninety-nine percent of the parents were single/divorced women. The needs of the girls were primary. Through working with the girls, the counselors found a real problem that had to be addressed before they could help the girls. That was the problems of the mothers. That is when we established a *"Grandparent"* support group. Can you imagine a group of grandparents and the average age is 26–36? What a revelation! In the grandparent support group, we worked with the women on self-esteem, self-love, handling their teens and their own attitudes, problem-solving skills, parenting skills, communication skills, etc. In addition, we had to work on their adjustment to becoming grandparents at such an early age. They were not prepared, mentally or financially. In most of these cases the mother was struggling to make ends meet. Suddenly, she had a teen who was pregnant, and no father to help because the father is a teen himself or just plain irresponsible. She is put upon to take care of herself, her daughter and a baby. Should she be resentful? Perhaps, but most of these women were committed to helping their daughters. They just needed some help themselves to be better prepared to help their daughters. Many of these women were just beginning to get their own lives together, when they were faced with trying to help a teen mother who had neither the expertise nor the means to raise a child. That old saying about "children raising children" was certainly true. The other problem, in most cases, was no extended family to help. So for those of you who may say, as many have said to me, *"my grandmother was married at thirteen and had 10 children by the time she was 26 and she raised them with morals and values."* I say to you yes, those were different times. 9 out of

10 times, the husband was also there helping to raise his children. The extended family was intact. Everyone, including teachers and neighbors, took responsibility for children. It is not that way today.   A woman heads Four out of five households in this country.   And a large percentage of those households live below the poverty level.   It is a different situation and a different time in history. This is not a black, white or yellow problem; this is a national problem.

Let's Discuss The Absent Parent

After my divorce, I decided that I was going to be both mom and dad to my children. I promised myself they would never want for anything. They didn't want for anything – materially, that is. But, the thing they needed most was their father's love and they did not get it. They blamed me. That seems unfair, huh? Well, it is the truth. Perhaps because I did not share my pain or my fears with them. I presented them with an "I can handle anything attitude." They were not aware of the tears and pain because I hid them. I thought the fact that I stepped up to the plate and took care of them was enough. It wasn't. I was careful not to put their father down. But I did nothing to bring them and their father together. He did nothing to make sure he was a part of their lives, and I let him get away with it. Ladies, we cannot be father and mother. We can try to be the best mother we can possibly be, but children need their father. You may not need him, but they do. They need and want his presence, his love, his attention, and his support.   We are usually only concerned about his support-child support payments, that is. And we should be. He should be financially responsible for his children. But, if he is not or cannot be, that doesn't change the fact that the children want and need him in their lives. So if you find yourself in this situation, make your decision based on the needs of the children, emotional needs rather than financial needs alone. When you say to children, *"your father doesn't care about us, he doesn't send any money,"* what they hear is *"I'm bad"* or *"I did something wrong because daddy doesn't love me anymore."* They do not have the reasoning skills of an adult, so they cannot evaluate things the way you do. No matter how well you believe you can explain it to them, they still blame themselves. So, ladies, if he is willing, let him spend time, even when he is not spending money. I know I will hear from some of you on this one, but I am more concerned about our children's self-esteem, and their being able to love themselves, than I am about trying to prove who is right.

I was sitting in the Movie Theater, I liked the movie, but there was a part that sent cold chills down my spine. What bothered me even more is that in all of the discussion groups I have participated in, with both men and women, no one else seemed to be bothered by this single line, that to me was one of the biggest misconceptions in our society today. It was the scene near the end of the movie, when "Russell" (played by Leon) returned to his lover "Robin" (played by Lela Rochon) only to discover she was pregnant. Throughout the movie, she had played an airhead. Suddenly she was this newfound woman and proudly announced to him as he backed out the door, *"I want you to read my lips, we (meaning she and the baby) don't need you in our lives."* Then she slammed the door in his face and returned to the couch and continued reading the baby book of names and let out a victorious--Yes!!!. The wave of applause that irrupted from the audience also upset me. The squeals, screams and the *"you go girls"* signified their approval of her attitude. But, what concerned me more was the approval of her rejection of the baby's father. I thought to myself, wait a minute, you may not need him, but his baby certainly does. I knew at that point that I would be addressing this issue in my book. I talk about it every chance I get with women and children—and even men when I get a chance. I know that children need their father as much as they need their mother. Not just for a paycheck or for child support or a gift at Christmas or on birthdays. But, a father who can say *"I Love You"* in words as well as actions. It doesn't matter what has happened to the relationship between that man and woman. We are talking about the relationship of the parent and child. No one parent can give children what they need emotionally. Children need both of their parents to love them, guide them, and teach them to love themselves. Their identity is tied up in their parents until they become teens. Then their pain often shows up in their acting out. As a professional speaker, I speak to poor people, wealthy people, white people, black people, all people, and I hear similar stories. Race, social status, economics have nothing to do with it. Unless we all realize and recognize what has gone terribly wrong with our children, we will all suffer as a society.

Single moms, please understand I am not blaming you. I am not criticizing you. I am one of you. I am certainly not suggesting that every wrong thing your child does is your fault. Please understand we are in this together. I suffered the same pains and made some of the same mistakes you made. I know your plight and I sympathize with it. But I also know the plight of our children. I have heard their cries for help. I have learned to recognize the cries through the work that I do. So I believe it is incumbent upon me to pass this knowledge on to you in this book. The suicide rate among teens is alarming. Teens are having babies they neither want nor can afford to have. Children are using drugs at an earlier age than ever before, and the drugs are more potent and more dangerous than ever before. We are talking about our futures. Mothers, if we are to have a future, if our children are to have a future, we have to become emotionally and spiritually healthy so that we can help them heal.

Save The Children

I was invited by Centinnel High School to speak at a tribute ceremony for Corrie Williams, the young child shot and killed on an MTA bus in Los Angeles, and for Ennis Cosby, the son of actor Bill Cosby. The auditorium was packed with teachers, students and their parents. The Corrie Williams family, and a family who had also lost a son, were present. I want to share with you portions of the speech I shared with them that day. This speech evoked so much emotion from the kids. I want you to know the kids recognize the problems. They just don't know what to do about it. They acknowledge their pain, their disappointment in us, their resentment of us and their lack of self-love and respect. They know we (society and adults in general) have failed them and they want to hold us accountable. They are doing that the only way they know how. By acting out and being destructive to themselves. The topic of the speech was self-love and self-respect. I said:

"...We have sent you the wrong message. We told you that worth is measured by: the car you drive, the home you live

in, the clothes you wear, your 'status' in life. Our message has been very clear and very well received. If your car is not expensive enough, your home is not big enough, your clothes are not of a designer brand, then you are <u>nobody</u>. And we wonder why you will rob, steal, even kill to acquire these things. Whatever happened to 'a man is not judged by the suit he wears, but by the content of his character?' We must change the message. Put us on the spot. Make us give you answers, the truth. I know you've been disappointed. I know you've been let down. I know you've been misled, mistaught. I know you are looking for answers. Make us accountable to you for the answers   We know you've been looking for answers. You deserve answers. You see we were given the wrong message and we passed it on to you. But its time for us to change the message..."

The children stood up applauded, whooped and whistled. They were glad to hear an adult express out loud what they felt inside. There were Blacks, Whites and Latino children that came up to me afterwards and expressed how they felt hearing their pain expressed out loud by an adult. How they were motivated by what I said. How they were willing to work to try and find an answer. We have to help them find the answers. They cannot do it without us.

A Mother's Prayer By: Linda Coleman-Willis

God,

Through all that I do, all that I might do, and all that I possess, I ask that I project an image that my children and their children will be proud to duplicate.

Through my continued show of faith, I pray that I can strengthen theirs, and help them develop their own pathway through life.

If at any time I have failed or shall fail them, give them wisdom enough to know human error in judgment, not malice, is the order of the day.

Through gathered knowledge and gained experience, I pray that I can help them grow and develop their talents, their desires and help them to overcome their obstacles and accept their limitations.

Through expressed love, unlimited patience and a total commitment, I ask that you help me to teach them to strive for happiness and peace. In Jesus name I pray.

Chapter 6

How to Create the Life You Want

Get rid of those old worn-out ideas that are not working anymore. We are governing our lives today by ideas and beliefs that we learned in the past. Most of these ideas and beliefs were given to us by other people. They are not our ideas or beliefs. Perhaps they worked for other people, but they certainly are not working for you. Reexamine your beliefs. Ask questions. We experience things by how we interpret them. If we want to examine our ideas and beliefs, we must take a look at how we interpret events. Don't make hasty judgments. Think about an incident, one that you would usually assign an explanation to without thinking about it. Try looking at it from a different perspective.

Our moods, outlook and attitudes are governed by the interpretation we give to events. So, if we hastily assign negative explanations, we are creating a negative attitude, mood or outlook for ourselves. All I am saying to you is to reexamine how you interpret things. Use logic and facts, instead of reverting back to using past judgments and feelings. Make sure you are not using old, worn, outdated information, excuses, feelings and ideas to make current decisions. We do it without realizing it because it is a habit. We are trying to run our lives with what I call useless-information. We have not stopped to examine it for its worth and value to us. We have not attempted to discard it for new information. We have not questioned it, because it is the status quo.

If you have lived a quarter century or more, you need new information. You need to reexamine what ideas and beliefs you are allowing to govern your life. A lot of what we have learned is not working for us. We can unlearn helplessness, worry, hate, and pessimism. We can unlearn anything that is not working for us.

EXERCISE

Re-examine your beliefs. Ask questions. Get away from the status quo.

Is this idea or belief working for me?

Is it as viable today as it was when I adopted it?

Do I need new information?

Is my interpretation of this event correct?

(If your answer to any one, or all of these questions, proves you need new information, or you need to change a belief, go to work immediately to try something new.)

Identify the areas in your life in which you are experiencing the most difficulty.

What can you do differently?
What resources do you need?
Who can help?
How can you change your thoughts? Actions? Beliefs?

Excuses: The "Yeah-Buts" of our Lives

Excuses are the explanations we give ourselves for why things turn out the way they do. If we are giving ourselves poor excuses, we are leading a poorly executed life. Because we are letting ourselves off the hook. Quality excuses lead to a quality life. If we excuse away our faults rather than attempt to change them, we will allow them to sabotage our progress. But, if we look at our faults and say these are my weaknesses and, instead of making excuses for them, identify them and take full responsibility for them and make a commitment to change them. This will increase our chance for a quality life. We empower ourselves, and we learn we can change for the better. But, as long as we make excuses for staying the same, we are closing the door on progress.

I call excuses the "Yeah buts." Every time we use "Yeah, but " before a sentence an excuse follows. It may be a good excuse, but it is still an excuse. Try to examine your excuses for legitimacy and necessity. Do you really need an excuse, or do you need an answer, an action step or a new explanation? Excuses are reasons for not doing what we should be doing. Do you want reasons or do you want successes? If we eliminate the reasons (excuses), we are left with successes. Don't accept any excuse, no matter how good it sounds, if it does not empower you to do better. Put the responsibility where it belongs, no matter how hard that may be or how much it hurts. In the long run, it will benefit you tremendously.

If you are going to give yourself excuses, give quality excuses. Instead of *"I never have enough time"* or *"There are not enough hours in the day,"* say *"I did not complete that task because of lack of planning. But, I am practicing time management from now on so I will have enough time."* Remember you recreate yourself by creating a quality life for yourself, and you create a quality life by examining and unlearning habits, ideas and beliefs that are not working. You have that kind of power. You can change your life because you can change how you think, how you process information, and the quality of your excuses. The hardest thing you will ever do is to get past old habits, old ideas, old beliefs, old failures-and old, tired, worn-out excuses. But, I guarantee you the effort is worth it. Your whole life will change.

EXERCISE

Rid yourself of excuses. Write down something you really want to do, but you are not doing it. Write down all the reasons you have for not doing it. Now look at those reasons, and understand they are only excuses. After each reason (excuse) write down ways you can eliminate that excuse. **Example:** 1. I want to be a speaker. 2. Reasons I am not speaking: I need training, etc. 3. Eliminate the reason(s): I need training--call toastmasters or a speech coach or a junior college for communication classes, etc. I think you get the idea. Now you try it. Remember: When you hear *"Yeah But"* there is usually an excuse following. In this exercise we are getting rid of all excuses, and then you are left with successes.

_____

_____

_____

_____

_____

_____

_____

_____

_____

Attitude: The Way We Think, Feel and Act

We create our own lives with our ideas and actions, and they can lead to great success or to frustration and disappointment. We all want success in our lives. And we can have it with the right attitude. Attitude encompasses our actions, feelings and moods. We can control our actions, feelings and moods; therefore, we can control our lives.

A positive attitude empowers us. We see possibilities-not just problems. Most people believe attitudes just happen. They don't. Attitudes are formed by the thoughts we hold in our minds over a period of time. These attitudes become the blueprints for our lives. Negative attitudes, full of fear, doubt and worry, reinforce negative behavior. But thinking positively creates positive attitudes, responses and feelings.

It's not easy to change our negative attitudes. It takes time. It takes practice. It requires stepping out of our comfort zone, and allowing ourselves to be uncomfortable. But the joy and success we experience when we act instead of react, when we see opportunity instead of problems, when we see possibility instead of impossibilities, is the greatest gift we can give ourselves and the people around us.

This ability to choose our thoughts, and thereby control our attitude, is one of our greatest assets. Positive thoughts produce a positive attitude thereby producing positive results. Negative thoughts produce a negative attitude thereby producing negative results.

Some experts say we have 450,000 thoughts per day and most are negative. In fact, one survey revealed that less than 5% of our adult population could identify which kind of thoughts they had, positive or negative. Imagine what our life would be like if 90% of those thoughts were positive instead of negative. Unfortunately, unless you have worked on yourself, a large percentage of those thoughts are negative. It is not so important that we have negative thoughts. That is natural. The long-lasting, harmful effect is our tendency to hang on and justify those thoughts. There is no negative attitude that the human mind cannot justify as being right. Fear, doubt, worry and hate are the basis of just about every negative attitude.

We can change our negative attitudes to positive ones. We can control our reactions to life's situations by controlling our thinking in a positive way. We can deliberately feed our minds with positive information. Replace fear with faith, doubt with determination, worry with work and hate with love. Read positive books, listen to tapes, take classes, go to seminars, and surround yourself with positive people. When you catch yourself putting yourself or others down, stop yourself immediately. Remember, whatever you say to or about others, effects you because, whether they hear you or not there is one person that will always hear what you say and that person is you. The way you verbalize effects the way you think and act. Our minds and bodies react to words. Either we control our words or they control us. When we use negative words they cause us to do negative things, but words used positively build up self-confidence. They create a positive, successful, happy and healthy life.

So you see words can effect us negatively or positively. They can effect our nervous system. Notice when you yell at someone how upset you feel. When you get angry with someone, your body feels the anger, perhaps more so than the person you are angry with. It is your nervous system that is reacting to all this anger, and it is not healthy. It is the words that you are using that disrupt your peace and the harmony in your body. Have you ever noticed how weak you feel after you have lost your temper? Being negative burns more energy than being positive. So, since we know we have a choice why not choose a positive, optimistic attitude?

Eliminating Negative Self Talk

So, for your own health and well-being take a look at how you are *"talking to yourself in your own mind."* When you do something that is not so smart, are you still saying things to yourself like, *"You are so stupid." " You never do anything right"?* Your body responds to your own voice. So if you call yourself stupid, your brain will believe you. It is far better to say *"that was not a smart thing to do. Let's not do it again."* Your brain will agree with you, and the next time you get ready to do that not so smart thing, your brain will remind you of what you said, and you will at least think about it before you repeat that not so smart thing. Practice eliminating any negative conversation you have with yourself by stopping it as soon as you are aware of it, and replacing it with a positive statement as I did in the previous example. I know this sounds a little far-fetched to some of you. But what do you have to lose by trying it? And, you have everything to gain.

So how do we eliminate negative self-talk? First, we have to acknowledge that it exists. Remember the survey revealed that less than 5% of the adults surveyed could identify which thoughts they had, positive or negative. But now we know that negative thoughts foster worry, tension, failure, frustration, dissatisfaction, unhappiness, even sickness. Positive thoughts foster success, happiness, growth, love, security, achievement, inner-peace, energy and health. It is the results we are getting that helps us determine which thoughts are most prevalent in our minds. Second, think about or write down how you feel in certain circumstances. Self-talk is measured by outcome, results. If you are not achieving the results you want, there is probably something there, holding you back. Remember, we all have a purpose and the ability to achieve that purpose. But, we may have to get our minds uncluttered first. What is your conversation with yourself when things happen to you that are within your control? That is out of your control? How do you view Risk? Responsibility? Can you dare to be different? Third, get in the habit of deliberately quoting positive affirmations, reading positive books, listening to motivational tapes. If you are spiritual, read scriptures and speak positive, uplifting words. Fourth, never listen to the news just before going to sleep, unless of course it is *"good news."* And finally, you can control negative self-talk by talking out loud to yourself. You respond to your own voice. If you feel uncomfortable talking to yourself, record your voice on tape. You can record your affirmations and listen to them just before falling off to sleep. This is a powerful exercise. Have you ever found yourself humming a tune that you heard days ago? It stuck in your mind, and you are still humming it. Your goals and affirmations can have the same effect on you. Affirmations are positive declarations. They are a great way to start and end each day. The effect this will have on your mental thoughts will thereby effect your attitude.

Create and record your own affirmations, or write them down and read them. Begin each sentence with *"I."* Some examples of affirmations are: *"I am energized by my goals, dreams and ambitions." "I am filled with vitality, energy and a healthy consciousness." "I hold only good, positive thoughts in my mind, knowing they will be expressed in my life." "I am in complete control of my actions and my thoughts." "I am conscious only of the good in others." "I let go of all limiting thoughts of fear, worry, and doubt." "I love myself unconditionally."*

The kinds of thoughts you allow to penetrate your mind, and the quality of people you surround yourself with, greatly influences your life. So surround yourself with positive people. Stop all criticism. Praise yourself for having the guts to try. Be gentle and kind and patient as you are learning a new way of thinking. Treat yourself as you would your best friend or anyone else you really love. Be kind to your mind and allow only positive thoughts to enter. At least once a day, say to yourself, *"I love You"* and *"I accept you just as you are"* Pretty soon, you will feel it. It will be evidenced by all the wonderful things happening in your life.

Creating A Positive Self-Image

How do you look at your self, through your strengths or through your limitations? Most successful people look at themselves through their strengths. Successful people build on their strengths rather than being overly concerned about their limitations. We all have limitations. Having them is not important; it is how we respond to them that is important. Are you allowing them to hold you back? Are you denying them and running away from them? Are you allowing them to control your life?

People have achieved great success because of the way they have responded to their limitations. A blind, retarded man with no formal training, can play any song on the piano after hearing it only once. A young girl whose legs were badly crippled by a childhood disease becomes a world-renowned dancer. A woman confined to a wheel chair becomes a world class athlete. A woman with one leg learns to ski and competes in ski competitions. Now, if these people overcame their disabilities and setbacks to become high achievers, think of the possibilities for your life. We are not stuck with the way we are. We can change. We can overcome any challenge with the right attitude. Face your limitations as challenges and use them to grow strong. Facing your limitations can give you confidence and personal satisfaction.

If you can see it, you can be it. If you believe it, you can achieve it. In order for you to develop a quality life, you must be able to see yourself living it. We have to be able to visualize our own capabilities. We have to have a clear, positive self-image. Self-image, the image you have of yourself, governs your life. If you cannot see yourself doing something, you literally cannot do it. But self-image can be changed. We can shape our ideal image of ourselves by looking beyond who we are to who we can become. We can envision ourselves doing what it is we want to do. This is called visualization. When visualizing, seek total relaxation. Then place the vision in your mind, and hold it there for at least 30 seconds. Eventually hold it for 60 seconds, and even longer with practice. Remember, *what the mind can conceive and believe, you can achieve.* Hold that vision of accomplishment, attainment, satisfaction before you, every chance you get. Think about it the first thing in the morning and the last thing at night before going to sleep. Dream about it, plan for it, because it is yours.

Using your strengths to improve your own self-image requires acceptance of the things you cannot change, changing the things you can and the wisdom to know the difference. Look and feel your best, not for the sake of other people, but to enhance the image you hold of yourself. Get involved in developing yourself. Read books that inspire and motivate, listen to tapes, take classes, go to seminars, take up hobbies, surround yourself with positive people. Expecting yourself to be perfect all the time is a setup for failure, but expecting to improve and become better is a commitment to your own improved self image.

EXERCISE

Make a Positive Inventory List. Write down only good, positive things about yourself. Include your abilities, talents, accomplishments, physical appearance, character, family, and goals. Look at yourself through the eyes of a friend or lover. Read this list every time you start to feel bad about yourself. This will help shape your ideal image of yourself. Look beyond who you are to who you can become. Do not expect yourself to be perfect all the time, but expect to get better.

Create your personal affirmations, beginning with *"I am,"* or *"I can."* Write them on a small card, or record them on a cassette and carry them with you. Imbed the affirmations in your subconscious by repeating them at least three times a day.

Create your visualization. If you can see it, you can be it. See yourself doing or having whatever you want. Some people tell me they are not good at visualizing. Try a familiar object first—an apple or an orange or a flower. Close your eyes. Relax and take a deep breath. Clear your mind. Now see the object. Keep putting it back into your mind until it is very clear. Another way to sharpen your visualization skills is to look at the flame of a candle until you can close your eyes and see it. Once you can see it, keep it focused directly in front of you. Do not allow it to float off to the right or left. Keep practicing until you get it. The results will be well worth the effort.

AFFIRMATIONS

"Read them in good faith that your lives may be transformed."

(For Prosperity)
Infinite Spirit, open the way for my right home, my right friend, my right position. I give thanks that it now manifests under grace in a perfect way.

(For Right Conditions)

Divine Love now dissolves and dissipates every wrong condition in my mind, body and affairs. Divine Love is the most powerful chemical in the universe, and dissolves everything which is not of itself.

(For Health)
Divine Love floods my consciousness with health, and every cell in my body is filled with light.

(For Guidance)
I am divinely sensitive to my intuitive leads, and give instant obedience to Thy will.

(For Right Work)
I have a perfect work (business) in a perfect way; I give perfect service for perfect pay.

(For Faith)
As I am one with God, I am one with my good; For God is both the Giver and the Gift. I cannot separate the Giver from the Gift.

(For Freedom from all Bondage)
I cast this burden on the Christ within, and I go free.

Linda Speaks: On Motivation and Success

I am often asked what motivates you? How do you stay motivated? Where did your motivation come from? How did you become so successful?

Because I get these questions so often, I will attempt to answer them here. I am and was a lot like many of you. As women, we usually did not have anyone in our intimate circle of friends that had the answers to these questions. There were successful women, but with lots of challenges in their personal lives. So to answer these questions, let me start from the beginning.

First, I believe I have always had a unique philosophy about life. And that unique philosophy came from my parents. There were five of us children, and we were all taught that if we wanted something in life we could get it by working for it. I saw my parents working their own businesses back in the days when it was still very difficult for African-Americans in this Country. My father, having one son and four daughters, worked hard to impress upon us that we could do anything we wanted to do. That gender or color should not be used as an excuse or a handicap. My father was always in business for himself. He owned a grocery store, a hotel, a nightclub, the vending machines in our school and had two taxi cabs in the local cab company. In those days the taxicabs were privately owned. Today he would be called an *"entrepreneur,"* back then he was called a *"hustler."* In those days the ideal situation was to get a job, any job. My father never worked for anyone else. He always worked for himself. My father was before his time. My mother, even today, works for herself and has for the past fifteen years.

Philosophy, to me, means a way of life. The way I think. My belief system. The reasoning and logic behind how I live my life, the choices I make. I had the philosophy, but I did not always have the confidence. Because I did not have the confidence, I did not always do the things that would have or could have brought me success. Lack of confidence can be a huge obstacle. An obstacle we must continue to fight to overcome. If we have the talent and no confidence, we may never do anything with the talent.

The confidence came years later. That's another story. But, having the philosophy, I managed my personal and professional life by those standards. Whether I worked as a secretary or a bartender or a cocktail waitress, I had the same *"I am somebody"* philosophy. People noticed it and often commented on it. It attracted people to me and it made a difference in my life. It was easy to stand out because most people take on the attitude of the position they have in life. In other words, if they are the presidents of a company, they carry themselves differently than if they are the president's secretaries. My philosophy was just the opposite.

I don't remember exactly when or where I picked it up, but it worked for me. That philosophy was to look at the people who were above me in position or status. See how they dressed, how they acted, what they did for lunch, their philosophy about work, about life and adopt their philosophy. Notice, I did not say you had to be like them or look like them. For clarification I said *"adopt their philosophy."* Their way of thinking. Their way of doing things. The way they carried themselves. Their way of being. I didn't have a name for what I was doing, but I knew it worked. Today there is a fancy name for it. It's called "Modeling." Look at someone who is successful doing what you want to do, and model the behavior and the attitude. Anthony Robbins is famous for teaching this technique. But, in order to model someone, you have to be around her or have access to them. But, if you adopt "modeling" as a philosophy, make it a way of life. Make sure you are modeling people whose philosophy coincides with your own. This is a powerful technique and it works.

Don't hang around with secretaries just because you are a secretary. Don't dress and act like a secretary unless of course you want to remain a secretary. Dress and act like your boss or your boss' boss. Don't just go to lunch with the other secretaries, or people on your level or below. Make friends of some higher-ups. I tried it on several jobs and was promoted so quickly I made enemies of some of the people I left behind. That was not my intent, but it happened because they did not understand the "philosophy" behind my success. It was easier to envy me than to try and find out what I was doing and do the same thing.

Please understand, there is nothing wrong with being a secretary or any honorable (legal) profession. My point is, if you are aspiring to get ahead, you have to see how the people in the positions you are aspiring to behave. That brings me to another philosophy of mine. I adopted this one for myself. I am always aspiring to get to the highest level in whatever profession I am in. It doesn't matter what that profession is. I have my eye on the top. My philosophy is, if you are going to do it, be the best. The only way to be the best is to beat the best. The only way to beat the best is to know why they are the best. What is it that makes them the best. Emulate that. Create your own style, but adopt the qualities that will make you a success in your chosen field. Adopt the philosophy of successful people. Otherwise, you are following people who don't know any more than you do. You are following followers.

Another philosophy that I learned from the book *"Laws of Success"* by Napoleon Hill, helped me tremendously in real estate. The one law that seemed to springboard me to success was the law of *"doing more than you are paid."* Put another way, it is the law of *"increasing returns."* I know this is hard for the person whose philosophy is *"pay me more, then I will do more."* That is not the way it works. If you practice this law, it won't be long before you are paid for more than you do. Notice I said *"Practice."* Not read, think about or say *"I agree with that."* You must put it into practice in everything that you do, every chance you get.

The other practice that helped propel my real estate career was a practice called *"Hard Work."* Ever heard of it? In the early years, I worked 10 and 12 hours a day. Then I discovered a concept called *"Working Hard"* on me, on my attitude, on my thinking, on my beliefs. We formed a *"Master Mind"* group at the real estate office where I worked. We met every day for months from 6am to 8am. We used *"Laws of Success"* as our training guide. We went through the book one chapter at a time, learned each of the laws and began immediately to put them into practice in our lives. Some of the most successful Realtors in the Los Angeles area were a part of this group. So, what am I telling you? Hard work is important. There has never been a time when I did not have to work hard to be successful. But, there came a time when working harder on me, than on my career, paid big dividends. Working harder to develop you pays off much more handsomely than working to develop a career.

Anyone can adopt these philosophies. They are universal laws. They are available to anyone, and they work. These are not my laws, and they don't work for some and not for others. They work for all of us all the time if we practice them all the time. So you see, anyone can be successful if they know what to do. There are no secrets to success, only laws and a commitment to the process.

Are you willing to make the commitment? Are you willing to adopt a new philosophy? Are you willing to step outside of your comfort zone and try something new? Please don't tell me you are too old or it is too late. Are you still breathing? I believe the best teacher is show, not tell. I believe the best lessons are lived and not just learned.

I stay motivated by listening to other motivational speakers like Les Brown. I also stay motivated by motivating other people though live presentations, my audio and videotapes and writing this book. I am motivated by the thousands of people I speak to every year. Remember, I have been involved in personal development since 1981. After a while these laws and philosophies take over your inner thought process, eventually evidencing their presence in your outer life. You will hear this statement throughout this book. *"If you want to change your life, change your thinking."* Up until now maybe it was just another cliché or a cute saying. But, I hope you realize the importance of the statement and make every effort to make it a reality in your life. Success leaves clues, lots of clues, but we have to be smart enough and alert enough to pick them up.

Success in life is very simple all you need to do is:

1. Get absolutely clear on what it is you want in your life, in your relationships, and in your career.

2. Develop a plan on how to achieve it. Role model successful people. Who do you know who is already getting that result? Do what they do. What do they do every day? What is their attitude about success?

3. Master your energy level and find a way to increase it. Keep it high.

4. Cultivate faith and belief in yourself, in your abilities. Do that through affirmations and prayer. Create a daily ritual for increasing faith and belief. Example: an affirmation, *"Day by day, in every way I am getting better and better."* Or a spiritual prayer: *"As I am one with God, I am one with my good."*

5. Take action. Massive action. Consistent, deliberate action every day. Nothing happens, until you do something.

Answer the following questions--What Do I Want In My Life:

1. Personally?

2. Emotionally?

3. Spiritually?

4. Financially?

5. Physically?

6. Professionally?

7. Family?

Chapter 7

Developing Personal Power

We must be willing to work harder on ourselves than on anything or anyone else. In order to become all we want to be, we must develop ourselves. We cannot leave it up to anyone else, nor can we leave it to chance. We must be responsible for developing ourselves. I am talking about more than education, more than physical exercise. These things are important, but I am talking about developing the inner self. The inner self consists of spiritual, emotional, and the psychological self. The inner self will take us through the tough times. That self that is sacred and hidden from the world. That self that is responsible for our thoughts, our doubts, our fears. It is when we develop the inner self that we really begin to grow and experience success and happiness. Inner growth and development creates inner peace, harmony and strength.

To develop the inner self, we must examine every aspect of our lives, our thoughts, and our existence. Everything we have ever seen, heard, felt or thought about is stored in our subconscious minds. Some of us are running our lives today off of outdated, useless information, possibly stored in our subconscious minds since childhood. Can you imagine an adult woman using skills learned from childhood to solve problems she has today? It happens every day. But, we are not aware of it. All we know is our lives are not working. We don't know why. Examine the actions and attitudes of a child when they want something. They want it now. They don't think about the consequences of having it. They don't care whether it's good or right for them. They want it and they want it now. They are not concerned about upkeep or maintenance or being responsible. They throw temper tantrums. They hit, throw things, stomp, yell and scream. Sound like some adults you know? Does it sound like you? Are you still handling your problems as an adolescent would? Have you moved past your childhood skills into adult skills of coping and handling challenges? If not, you are probably wondering why your life is not working. I believe if we consciously examine our habits, beliefs and actions, we will discover some of the sources of our problems. We talked about habits and beliefs in the prior chapters. Let's talk about actions in this chapter.

Personal Development Is The Key

Since I started personal development 15 years ago I have become very observant both of my own life and the lives of others. It is easy for me to make the comparison, because I have done so much work on myself. I am not better, just more informed and enlightened. It is a journey I encourage everyone to take. It will make a difference in your life. It takes time, and commitment to a different way of doing things, and a new way of thinking, but it is worth it. Your life will change.

Think about this for a moment. What do you have today that you had 15 to 20 years ago? Do you still wear the same clothes, drive the same car, and live in the same place? Most of you will probably answer no to at least two out of three of these questions. You don't have those things because you made a conscious decision to change them, to get rid of them, to replace them. Have you made a conscious decision to change your mind? To change the way you think? To rid yourself of all that old, outdated, useless, misguided information that served you 15 to 20 years ago, or even 5 to 10 years ago, but definitely is not serving you today? Are you consciously upgrading your inner world as you upgrade your outer world? Are you moving forward mentally as you move forward physically?

You cannot have a successful adult relationship acting like a child. You cannot expect an adult relationship to flourish if you behave like a child. We must examine our attitudes and behaviors to see if we have matured sufficiently to handle relationships. If not, then we need to work on ourselves before we enter into a mature relationship. This may require professional assistance. This is not a dirty word. We go to a doctor when we are ill. We go to the dentist when we have a toothache. Why don't we seek professional assistance when we have an emotional problem? Perhaps some of us are still in the dark ages. Getting professional help suggested some dark taboo about mental illness. Today there are competent therapists who can assist you in handling your emotional problems. Get a referral. Find someone who you feel comfortable with. Find someone who shares your values. Talk to them and get to know how they work and if that fits with how you want to be treated. It is important that we learn to take care of our emotional and psychological needs. We are taught to take care of our biological needs - food, clothing and shelter. But we are not taught to take care of our psychological needs-love-a sense of worth, of value, feeling like you count, like you really matter. two, security -- feeling like you have some control over your life, peace of mind; and, Fun-- excitement, and enjoyment. These are the basic psychological needs. We quite often leave the fulfillment of these needs to chance. Then there are our emotional needs. We need to feel needed, respected, admired, valued, wanted and appreciated. We tend to hide these needs, but they show up anyway in our relationships. So we have to make it ok to take care of our emotional needs in a healthy way.

To develop ourselves, the first thing we have to do is make a commitment to the process. How do we change after being the same way for so many years? By identifying the areas in our lives where we are having the most difficulty. By examining those areas carefully. Are we using information that is outdated? Do we need to learn how to handle our information differently? Do we lack the skills to handle this area effectively? If we are answering yes to these questions, we need to do the work. Then we have to learn everything we can about the process. What is it we need to do differently? What resources do we need? Who can help? Then we have to put what we learn into action. This is usually the hardest part. If we neglect to act, we will remain stuck in old habits and ways of thinking and living. Finally we have to face our fears. Fear will always be there; it is part of the bargain. But, we can learn to deal with our fears and continue to move forward. We cannot allow the fear to stop us. We have to face our fears and find ways to continue even in the face of fear and doubt.

What can we do to assure that we will continue to develop ourselves and continue to improve as time goes by? We need a master plan for our lives. We have to know what we want our lives to look like, to feel like. We have to know what we want to have in our lives. We need a personal development plan. A plan to make sure we improve as human beings. What is your life like right now? Is it what you want? Does it feel right? If you are answering no to these questions, you have work to do. If you answered yes, you still want to continue to grow and develop in a positive direction.

EXERCISE

Create A Personal Development Plan.   Answering these questions will help you create a personal development plan that you can follow to make the necessary changes. You may want to review it every two to three years for areas needing to be updated.

Personal Development Plan

What do you want to change or improve?

What new behavior/attitude do you want to develop? How will you go about it? Who can help?

What are your personal career objectives?

What new skills have you learned or need to learn?

What training, seminars, classes have you taken or need to take?

What books or professional literature have you read or need to read?

What networks or organizations do you belong to or need to join?

What are your plans for personal development in the next year? For professional development?

How can you apply what you have learned from this book to enhance your personal growth?

Write out a specific description of what your life would look and feel like if you could have it the way you wanted it to be right now. Describe what you would have in your life.

Where would you live?

How would you live?

What would you look like?

How would you talk?

How would you walk?

Who would you be around?

Who are your friends?

What is your income? Savings? Retirement?

Invest In Yourself

The greatest investment in the world is the investment you make in yourself. It is more important than any other you will ever make, except perhaps the investment you make in other people.   We tend to invest our time and money in asset building for material gain, and that is important. There are lots of good books out there to teach us how to do that. But, the biggest return on our money and time is the money and time we invest in ourselves

There is no higher return on an investment, than the return we get on our investment in ourselves and in other people. If we had a Wall Street for human investment or a stock market for investing in our future, we would never have a stock market crash. But hoping that someone else will invest in us is fruitless. Investing in ourselves is our best return on effort, time, energy and money. The next time you get ready to make a material purchase, ask yourself if this money couldn't be better spent on a book, tape, seminar, class or some personal development program. Ask yourself if you are investing enough in your personal development program. If you spend more on shoes every year than you do on books, you may not be.

Are you continuing to develop yourself every day, week, year, or are you allowing yourself to fall behind? We have to continue to invest in ourselves in order to continue to grow and develop as human beings. It is not a once and for all event. You cannot exist on yesterday's meal, neither can you exist on yesterday's knowledge. You must continue to develop yourself and to move forward. If you neglect to fertilize your mind, you are neglecting your future growth. Think about what happens when you neglect the grass. It turns brown and dies. Eventually, weeds overtake it, and before you realize it, there is no sign of grass. But, the minute you decide to cut it and water it and nurture it, the grass will return, and before long you will have a beautiful, well-kept lawn. But even then you have to continue to cut, water and care for it, so it will remain green. Any neglect, and it will return to its forlorn state. So it is with our minds. With our lives. Our lives are in ruins because we are not taking care. We are not watering and caring for ourselves the way we should. Everything else is more important. Working on a job that we hate. Paying bills for things we don't need. Buying stuff that we neither want nor can afford.

We go through life with this quiet hunger buried deep down inside of us, until we begin to forget about our dreams, our desires, and our goals. They are covered over, and unless we wake up somewhere down the road, we will lead dull, unhealthy, poor, miserable lives   We will never know the greatness that could be, should be, ours. We will go through life watching and wondering why some people seem to have good things happen to them while our lives are falling apart.

But I know, and I hope you know by now, that you can change all that. Your life can be whatever you decide it will be. It requires that you be honest with yourself and be willing to examine your choices. Take a look at what has led you to this point in your life because you are going to have to do something different to get to where you want to go.

Albert Einstein said, *"You cannot solve a problem at the same level in which it was created."* If you are not where you want to be in life you need to do something different. If you are getting small results, then you need to increase your efforts. If you want to develop yourself, you cannot do it on the same level at which you created this life. You have to rise to a higher level. You need additional training, perhaps some new information. You need to introduce something new or different into the equation. You can see better when you are up above something looking down on it, rather than viewing it at the same level, or from below . So we have to rise above who we are to become who we want to be.

Realize that if you don't invest in yourself, and work at developing yourself, you will never be any more than you are right now. Is that a scary thought? You can become all you were meant to be, if you will do all you can do to improve yourself. And all you can't do, find someone else who can. Be willing to ask for help. Be teachable. Be willing to learn from others. Invest in yourself and create a fantastic future. Invest in yourself and make this a better world. Invest in yourself and enjoy the returns on your investment. Invest in yourself and know that you can never lose your investment. The market will not crash. The value will not go down. Invest in yourself and you invest in your own potential for wealth, health and happiness. Invest in yourself because when your self-worth goes up, your net worth will go up.

Preparedness Meets Opportunity

I thank God every day for my life. I know it is so easy to make the wrong decisions in life. I have not always made the right decisions, but I have never given up. I know lots of people who have. Very capable, competent, gifted individuals. People with much more talent than I have. But, they were not willing to invest in themselves. It was more important to invest in things than in themselves.

Whitney Young Jr. said, *"It is better to be prepared for an opportunity and not have one than to have an opportunity and not be prepared."* When we invest in ourselves, our skills, our talents and our minds, our opportunities increase. We actually create opportunities by being prepared.

I can tell you a lot of stories about preparedness meeting opportunity in my own life. One of the most exciting stories is the time I received an invitation from Les Brown, one of the top motivational speakers in the country today, to participate in a self-empowerment conference in Nassau, Bahamas.

I could not hold back the tears. But they were tears of joy. I, Linda Coleman-Willis, an international speaker. I thought about all the sacrifices. All the times I thought this would never happen. The rejection, the disappointments, the setbacks, the cancellations, the broken promises, the doubt, the fear, the worry. I thought about all the times I had asked myself "Is It Worth It?" and the many times I had to convince myself that it was.

When we prepare ourselves, when we invest in ourselves, even when there is no promise of an opportunity in sight, we are expressing belief that it really can happen. We are increasing the chances that it really will happen. It won't always be easy, especially when we are feeling discouraged. But, remember if we do nothing, we are guaranteed it will never happen.

From the moment I started to make right decisions, my life started to change. It did not happen overnight, which is one of the reasons people have such a problem hanging on. They want instant change. But, it did happen. There were gradual changes. I also knew when I wasn't doing all I could, because the slowdown of progress was very evident. I could feel it and I knew I had to get back on track real fast.

Everything in life is cause and effect. This law of cause and effect works both ways. If you are causing bad things to happen, then you will reap bad things in your life. If you want something good to happen in your life, you have to cause something good to happen. There is only one foolproof way to know what we believe. That is to look at what we achieve. Then we know exactly what our beliefs are. The good news is if we are not happy with what we have achieved, we can change our beliefs to work with us instead of against us. That gives us the power to change whenever we are ready.

I have lived all my life for these moments in time. Now, I know what an Olympic champion feels like. They train all their lives for a twenty-second moment of glory. But, the victory lasts a lifetime. What you become as a result of the discipline and training lasts a lifetime. That moment of glory fades, but the growth, development and acquired abilities are yours to do with whatever you choose. No one can take that away from you. It is yours and you will never be the same person again. The growth, the development, the ability is your pay-off for being committed and paying your dues. These qualities can be applied to any area of your life for growth and development. The joy of having a dream come true is so satisfying.

I believe I have, as most people have, always known in my heart that I was special. But, because I did not hear it from other people, (and whether we want to admit it or not that is where a lot of our self-esteem comes), I did not believe I was special. I did not believe that I deserved the kind of life I secretly wished for. But, I know now that our lives are what our thoughts make it. We don't have to wait for anyone to make us feel special. We can do that for ourselves. That is now a personal ritual between God and me.. Create your own ritual for feeling special. I only think thoughts that coincide with what I want in my life. I want health, wealth, happiness, Godliness, peace on earth. I want to be an example to my family, and an inspiration to all people.

I am only one person, but I know one person can make a difference in the world. God created each of us with a specific purpose in mind. It is when we are living that purpose that we are at our best. It is when we recognize and accept that purpose that we experience Utopia. I am still awed by it all. Because I am doing what I love to do, I am living my purpose. I am living my dream. I decided to write this book two years ago. I started and stopped so many times.   There were always challenges, and reasons why I could not finish it. But, when I made a commitment and made it a priority and solicited support, it happened. We can do anything we want to do if we make a commitment to the process, focus and get the help we need.

Whatever it is you want to do, prepare for it. Start now, preparing. Remember what happens when you prepare. The only way to get a return on your investment is to invest the time, energy and money. Make the sacrifices. These are all down payments on your future. Remember, nothing happens unless you are preparing for it to happen, preparing to make it happen, or prepared when it happens. The key is preparation.

EXERCISE

My Daily Rituals

Begin with an affirmation:
"Today I choose to have a good day.   I will communicate confidence in everything that I do.   I will consciously look for the good in others and in myself."

Today I found myself thinking/feeling the following positive thoughts (Attitudes):

_____

_____

_____

_____

_____

Today I took the time to do the following **Just For Me**:

_____

_____

_____

_____

_____

Today I Improved my mind by:

_____

_____

_____

_____

_____

Today I took time to improve my physical self by:

_____
_____
_____
_____
_____
_____

Today I made someone else feel good by:

_____
_____
_____
_____
_____
_____

Self Empowerment is Personal Power

What is Empowerment: People feel empowered when they are energized by what they do. When you feel empowered, you have a sense of excitement, vitality and enthusiasm about what you are doing. You enjoy doing it, doing your best work, and learning more about it so that you can do it even better. The task nourishes and sustains you. By contrast, when you do not feel empowered by a task, you experience the task as uninteresting or even as drudgery, which drains you of energy. Empowerment can be situational.   You can feel relatively empowered on some tasks and in some areas of life, and can feel less empowered on others.

Four Feelings of Empowerment

In order to feel empowered there are four feelings that need to be present

1. Choice - The feeling of being free to choose, being able to use your own judgment and act out of your own understanding. We feel we are in control when we have the freedom of choice and this empowers us. But, we have to take responsibility for the choices we make. Making your own decisions on matters that are important to your task. Trusting your own judgment.

2. Competence - The feeling that you can do something well. That you are doing good quality work. That you are skillful. Appreciate your own success. Recognize what is going well. Acquire new skills and further develop old ones. Learn from other's successes without feeling threatened.

3. Purpose - The feeling of meaningfulness. You are doing something that is worth your time and energy. Feeling that you are on a valuable mission, that your purpose matters in the larger scheme of things. Understand your own values and passions. Create a vision that supports who you are.

4. Progress - is the accomplishment you feel in achieving something. It involves the sense that you are moving forward, that your activities are really accomplishing something. Look for ways to continuously improve your own performance. Take

time to stop and celebrate your milestones. Build collaborative relationships with others.

Personal development precedes personal achievement. If you want to achieve personal success, you must develop yourself. You must continue to develop yourself. The work on you is ongoing. I know people who are living their lives today based on ideas and lessons they learned years ago. Are you one of them? Remember we learned some of this stuff from people who didn't know any more than we did. We are still today allowing things from our past to dictate our future.

If you can read, you can learn. If you can listen, you can learn. If you can absorb information, you can learn. If you open yourself up to new experiences, to the possibility of seeing things from a different perspective, to the ideas and ways of life of people that are different from you, you can learn and grow and prosper in ways you never dreamed. This broadens our perspective of the world and ourselves. We suddenly realize that this narrow focus we consider our world is so much more and so much larger. There is a whole new world waiting for you if you dare to reach past the boundaries you have set for yourself. If you dare to stretch and grow.

You are going to feel some discomfort, some fear, some uncertainty, But, that is where the growth comes from. Out of our ability to survive the discomfort and growing pains. I do it constantly. I challenge myself to try something different every day. To not make decisions based on old information. To refuse to do something because that's the way I have always done it. It's a stretch, but in my opinion that's the only way to live. The only way to grow and get better at what you do.

Now, I am not talking about foolish decisions or irresponsible behavior. I am talking about doing something out of the ordinary for you. So that you can experience a life that is full of excitement, one that creates opportunity for growth in your personal and professional life.

Chapter 8

How To Make Better Choices

People make stupid choices in their lives; then they want to blame everyone else for it. We spend a great deal of our lives making the wrong choices and we wonder why our life is not working. If you make the wrong choice, at least try to learn from it and not make the same mistake twice. Our lives are what they are because of the choices we have made so far. The choices we make today will effect our lives five or ten years from now. If you want something different in your life, you must make some different choices. It is so important to happy, healthy, successful living that we learn to make better choices, that I dedicated a complete chapter to it. I would like to see a class in every school and every college on how to make better choices or on decision-making. Some people don't seem to know that it is the choices they make that get them into trouble.

They don't seem to know that they have a choice in life. That we always have a choice. We may not always like the choice, but we always have one.

Do We Really Have A Choice?

When you get up in the morning, you have the choice to have a good attitude or a bad attitude. You cannot control everything that happens to you during the day, but you can choose how you think about it, and therefore, how you feel about it, how you act or react toward it. So you have a choice. The question is, are you making the right choices? When someone says or does something to you that you do not like, you have a choice as to how to respond. You can choose to ignore it and walk away, or you can choose to say or do something about it. It is your choice.

When I speak to young people, and we have this conversation about choice, they often try to convince me that they don't have a choice in certain matters. They say things like *"I have to because of where I live"* or *"where I go to school"* or *"because my parents want me to."* Or, they will say, *"if some one makes me mad, I can't help it I have to react. I lose control."* So, I explain to them that the thought comes first, then the reaction. You can control your actions, because you can learn to control your thoughts. Sometimes it's hard for them to get the point, but I keep giving them scenarios until they understand they have a choice. For me it is very important that they understand they have a choice because when they realize this, perhaps one day they will be able to put it into practice.

Often in my seminars, I meet adults who will try to convince me that they don't have a choice. They say things like *"I have to go to work"* or *"I have to pay taxes"* or *"I have to pay my bills."* I say to them *"No, you don't, but, you may have to face the consequences of not doing those things."* But, you have a choice to do them or not do them; it is your choice. Most of us make our choices because of the consequences of not making those choices. It is so important that we get this point and not take it lightly, because we need to teach our children that they have choices. When they make good choices they have good lives, but when they make bad choices they suffer the consequences. We also need to teach them to make better choices and to be responsible for the choices they do make.

To Choose Or Not To Choose

Some people feel if they don't make a choice, they don't have to be responsible. But you are responsible anyway, because to not choose is to make a choice. You are always responsible for the choices you make or don't make, and no one else is going to take the responsibility, even if you wanted them to. You are responsible for the choices that you make in your life. If you don't like your life, change it by making different choices.

A choice to do something is a decision not to do something else. So be sure you are using your time wisely. That you are making decisions based on your goals. We can't do everything, so it is important that our choices are taking us in the direction we want to go. You must have a sense of purpose to achieve your goals. Choose roles, responsibilities and relationships that coincide with your goal, your purpose.

Decide you will be the best you can be at whatever you decide to do. That you are willing to expend the kind of time and money necessary to become the best. You are making choices based on what you want to happen in your life. You are not waiting, you are choosing, and you are making good, sound choices based on good sound information.

Unfortunately, in life we usually choose what we are rather than what we want or think we want. We cannot be anything more than our mental capacity allows us to be. If we are not constantly developing our minds, then we are struck with limited choices because we are stuck with limited thinking. Unless we are willing to learn new ways of doing and being, unless we are willing to work harder on us than on our jobs, unless we are willing to admit that we need new and different information, we will continue to make the same poor choices over and over. The good news is that we can choose to learn new and better information. We can decide that we want something different in our lives and make the decision to get it. We can take control of our lives and make a commitment to ourselves that we are going to learn whatever we need to learn to make our lives work.

We Become Our Choices

When I think of choices, I think of opportunity. I think of the ability to do with my life whatever I want. I think of possibilities. I think that I am becoming what I want to become because of the choices I am making, and I am making good, sound choices. Choices that coincide with what I want in my life, not what I don't want. I relish in the fact that the choice is mine to make and I can make whatever choice I want and that empowers me. I choose to live a happy, healthy, love-filled, prosperous, God-fearing life. I choose to love myself first so that I can love others. I choose what I want in my life and I choose to live a life that I am happy with. *I choose to grow from the joy of winning, not from the pain of losing. I choose to grow from inspiration, not from desperation. I choose to live by choice, not by chance.* I choose to be in control of my life instead of out of control. I choose my friends based on how I want to live my life. I am intentionally elevating the quality of people I allow to come into my life. It is my life and my choice. There is nothing wrong with selecting who your friends are. I respect all people, but all are not in my intimate circle of friends. We should choose our intimate circle of friends with care. Our friends reflect who we are or who we are becoming. We should never put down another human being, but we can choose not to allow that person or persons to bring us down. Choose your values and ethics and morals, and then only allow people with those same high standards into your inner circle. Somehow, we don't seem to understand how the company we keep effects our lives for good or bad.

Peer pressure is one of the most powerful forces in the world. For children and adults alike. Some adults are still making decisions based on what other people will say or think Their biggest fear is not being accepted. Some adults are still living their lives and making decisions based on the limited knowledge and beliefs they had as children. We see adults every day who have not grown up mentally. They act like children and are still using immature, childish, ideas and concepts to direct and control their adult lives. Therefore, their lives tend to resemble those of children. Uncontrolled, unstable, in a constant state of chaos. Our lives are a mess, because we are making choices and decisions that are not well thought out.

Before we make a decision we should ask ourselves several questions. How is this decision going to effect me? Will it be for good or ill? Am I making the best decision for myself or am I considering someone else's desires? How will this decision effect my life? Am I acting in my own best interest? What does this choice mean to me in the long run, will it help or hurt? Am I qualified to make this decision alone or do I need help? Am I willing to allow someone else to dictate how I make decisions or am I willing to take full responsibility for the choices I make? Do I want to live my life by choice, or by chance? If by chance, I will have to take whatever comes because I will have no control. Am I prepared to live a life without control? What do I want to teach my children about choices? Are making better choices important to me? Am I willing to learn to make better choices?

Choice, not chance, determines our lives. We must make a conscious decision to improve our lives. We must make a conscious effort to make better choices until it becomes second nature. Until it becomes a part of who we are, a part of our subconscious minds, and a way of life for us. I know you want a better way of life because you are reading this book.

It may surprise you that not everybody is willing to expend the time and effort necessary to create a better life. They won't read this book, or any book that can possibly help them to make better choices and better decisions in their lives. They will remain in misery, unhappy and unsuccessful all their lives, because they will not take the responsibility for what is happening in their lives and then take the necessary steps to change it. They will not make the choices and decisions that will make a difference in their own lives.

Obviously, you do not wish to be one of these people. I congratulate you on your courage and commitment to take action, because it is not easy to do something you have never done before. To take a look at your life and say *"I am not happy with where I am and I am going to do something about it"*. It takes courage to tackle change and determination to see it through. But, I believe you will see it through, because you are the person this book is written for. The person who is seeking and wanting to make a difference in her own life. A person who knows there is a better way and also knows it is her responsibility to find that better way. A person who has made the decision to do something about it. The person who is willing to admit what she doesn't know, and be willing to learn. You are the person who will see your life change for the better. You are not going through your whole life blaming something or someone else for your problems. You have resolved to do something about it, and you will. This book is for you.

I know what it feels like to want something better, but to be unsure how to get it. I know what it feels like to know that you deserve better, but to look around you and see people who either don't want more in their lives, or haven't a clue how to get it. I know what that is like. So if you are looking, you have found what you need. The words written on these pages are for you. The words are from my spirit to your spirit, because I believe there are no hopeless situations in life. No one is hopeless. Unless we give up on ourselves, we can always change our lives. It doesn't matter who gives up on us, as long as we don't give up on ourselves. It doesn't matter where you've been, it's where you're going that counts. Doesn't matter who you are, but who you have made up your mind to become. Doesn't matter what has happened to you up until this point in your life, what matters is what you are going to do about it now. It doesn't matter what other people think of you, what's important is what you think of yourself. What you think about who you are. What you are willing to do about what you want to become. It is your choice, your decision and your life.

How Do We Make Better Choices

We make better choices based on the poor choices we have made in the past. Look at your mistakes only for the lessons. Don't beat yourself up or put yourself down. Don't cloud your future by dragging past failures forward. Only bring yesterday's failures into today, if you can resolve them with today's solutions. Otherwise, leave them behind. Commit to making better choices. How do you make better choices?

1. Know the results you want. No one wants a bad life. We just fail to plan for a good one.
2. Get good information and feedback.
3. Don't rush blindly into situations or circumstances.
4. Be prepared.
5. Stop to think how an action is going to effect your life.

6. Set goals and make choices based on those goals.
7. Identify your purpose.
8. Create an action plan that coincides with your goals and your purpose.
9. Use the lessons you learned from making bad choices to make better choices.
10. Accept responsibility for what happens to you in life.
11. Become a seeker of wisdom and knowledge.
12. Work with a mentor who can direct you and help you make good choices.

EXERCISE

These are the questions from the chapter you just read. Now I want you to write out the answers to these questions in your journal. Answering these questions will help improve the quality of the choices you make.

Before making a decision, ask yourself the following questions:

1. How is this decision going to effect me in the long run?
2. Am I making the best decision for myself or am I considering someone else's desires?
3. How will this decision effect my life for the better? For the worse?
4. Am I qualified to make this decision alone, or do I need help?
5. Am I willing to take full responsibility for the choices I make?

6. What do I want to teach my children about choices?
7. Am I willing to learn to make better choices?

I_____ commit to the practice of making good choices in my life. I will practice by asking the questions found in this chapter before I make a choice. I am committed to improving my life by improving the choices I make.

Dated the _____ of _____.

_____
Signature

CHAPTER 9

Expand/Educate/Improve Yourself

If you want a better life, and I know you do because you are reading this book, you must expand, educate and improve yourself constantly. The world and everything in it is changing. We are no different. We must be moving forward, or we are going backwards. We cannot stand still, even if we want to. We not only have to expand our skills and talents, but we must expand and improve our minds. Education is important, but education alone is not enough. Think about a balloon. When you blow air into a balloon, it will never go back to exactly the same size again. So it is with your mind. Someone once said *a mind once stretched by a new idea will never be the same.* So we can educate ourselves, and that is a good beginning. But we must develop a personal growth program for ourselves.

After we graduate school, the work is just beginning. What we learn in school, even if we accomplish the highest level of academic achievement, it is usually not enough. We need to have a plan that will help us grow emotionally, mentally and spiritually. These are the things we just don't get in schoolbooks. The search to become the very best we can be is never ending. Jim Rohn is famous for saying *education will make you a living, but self-education will make you a fortune.* Even if you are only concerned with making a living, and not with making a fortune, you can improve the quality of your life by engaging in some form of personal development on an ongoing basis.

I was fortunate to interview Jack Canfield, author of *"Chicken Soup for the Soul,"* on my radio talk show *"The Motivation Power Hour."* We talked about personal development. Jack Canfield graduated from Harvard. When I asked him if he learned personal development through his formal education, he said no. He had to pursue it on his own after his formal education. Now, we all know Harvard is one of the best schools of higher education in the world. But they don't teach personal development and neither does any of the other excellent universities and colleges. Personal development is usually something we have to pursue on our own. But, no matter how well educated we are, we need to develop ourselves personally. Jack did say he learned something about teamwork because he was an athlete. But, it wasn't until he joined a group of individuals whose focus was on personal development, that he really learned what he needed to grow as a person.

The Key To Personal Power

Personal development is the key to personal power. We can achieve financial success, or success in other areas of our lives, and become very powerful. Money tends to give us power. But, personal development is the only way we will ever have personal power.

When I speak of personal development, I am talking about developing the mind, body and the spirit. I am talking about doing something that develops you, the person. If you want better muscles, you exercise your body. If you want a better life, you must fertilize your mind. We need skills in all areas of our lives. We need to know how to love ourselves and feel good about who we are. We need to know how to overcome obstacles in our lives. We need to know how to solve problems (problem solving skills are just as important today as knowing how to perform brain surgery), how to change our behavior, how to be responsible for our choices, how to develop ourselves in every area of our lives. I call these Life Skills. School does not teach us life skills. They do not teach us about relationships, with ourselves or with other people. If you have never played sports, you may not know about teamwork or leadership. It is a reality that we must work harder on ourselves than we work on our jobs. It is a reality that if we spend all of our time working on a job, and no time working on ourselves, the investment we will have made at the end of our lives will be equivalent to a gold watch. But, if we invest a small percentage of that time improving who we are, the return on the investment will be so much more. You will be able to measure it not only in monetary value but also in quality of life.

My Way Or No Way

The person who is closed to new experiences and new ideas has stopped growing. The "my way or no way" person has accepted a narrow view of life. We cannot grow, develop and experience personal success if we are stuck in self-righteousness. We have a choice to make. What's more important, being right or being happy? Is being right more important than learning, growing and improving? If you chose the latter, to expand, grow and improve, you are reading the right book. You are making the right choice. You are willing to open yourself up to new ideas and a different way of doing things. You are willing to experiment. Come down off your high horse and allow yourself to be vulnerable. Take a risk. The benefits are worth it. You will expand your mind, your life, your ideas and your attitude. Your outlook will change, your power will increase, and your life will take on new dimensions. You will be happier than you ever dreamed possible. Go ahead, try it. What do you have to lose compared with what you have to gain? When we expand, like the balloon filled with air, we can never be the same again. We are so much more. So much better. Our lives are so much richer. And the people around us are so much happier.

Self-righteousness is usually a cover up for insecurity. The need to always be right is a sign of doubt about our abilities. Explore this possibility. Examine your need to always be right. Is it a cover-up? Admitting it, identifying it and committing to change is the first step to a healthy you.

A self-righteous attitude says to other people "I am right, you are wrong." If you notice people avoiding you, or your employer writing on your evaluation *unable to get along with others,* you have probably crossed the threshold of being labeled an *"arrogant, opinionated, know-it-all."* People do not admire know-it-alls; they resent them.

Being right all the time is not possible. If you think you are right all the time, you can't learn anything new. Besides, being wrong sometimes means you are human. Make it ok to not know. If you don't know, say *"I don't know."* Practice these three little words. Use them occasionally to remind yourself you are a recovering *"Know It All."*

The next time you feel the need to prove you are right, ask yourself if being right is more important than the feelings of the other person, or the risk of creating resentment or isolation. Recognize and value other people's opinions. They may differ from your own, but that's ok. Remember what they say about opinions, *Everyone has one or two or three...*

Create A New Beginning

No matter what you want in life, you can have it because you can become it. It is yours if you can see it, smell it, taste it, hear it, feel it, hold it, caress it and cajole it. If you believe you deserve it, have faith that you can get it. No matter where you are in your life, you can recreate yourself. You don't have to go through life being and doing something you don't want to do and be. Stop right now and take a look at your life. What is it that you want that you do not have? What is it that you have that you want to get rid of? What is stopping you from doing it? You can create the self you want to be. You do not have to spend the rest of your life wishing. What do you want to become? Most of us have never asked these questions of ourselves. Most of us feel we are stuck with whatever we have, and we believe there is nothing we can do to change it. Most people settle in life. We settle because we don't believe we can have more, or we don't think we deserve it. When you love yourself, you know you deserve the best. When you know you deserve the best, you will only accept the best. When you only accept the best, you will become the best. It is a cycle. We can create what we want. It is not always obvious or easy, but it is possible.

I want you to pretend with me for a moment. Close your eyes. Relax and take a deep breath. Now I want you to see in your mind's eye what you would be doing right now if you could have whatever you wanted in life. If money, time, education were not factors What would you be doing right now? How would you look? What are you wearing? How do you sound? Where are you? Who is with you? What are they doing? Are you happy? Can you see it, smell it, taste it, hear it, feel it, hold it? Can you imagine it all being part of who you are? This is how people create. They see it in their own minds first. They can see it as clearly as you see the stars in the sky. They can taste it as certainly as you taste a piece of chocolate melting on your tongue. They smell it as strongly as you smell a cup of freshly brewed coffee. It is so real to them they can reach out and touch it. And they have faith and belief that they can have it. They know they are deserving of it, and they are willing to work for it, and they more often than not get it. This can work for all of us. But we have to first believe it, and then we have to take action. We have to love ourselves enough, believe in ourselves, and be willing to do the work to recreate ourselves to become the person we want to be.

EXERCISE

Practice the following exercise daily for 30 days. It is a very powerful visualization exercise.

Close your eyes. Relax and take a deep breath. Now I want you to see in your mind what you would be doing right now if you could have whatever you wanted in life. If money, time and education were not factors Hold this vision for at least 60 seconds.   Then answer the following questions.   Write the answers in your journal.

What would you be doing right now?
How would you look?
What are you wearing?
How do you sound?
Where are you?
Who is with you?
What are they doing?
Are you happy?
Can you see it, smell it, taste it, hear it, feel it, hold it?
Can you imagine it all being part of who you are?

Living Your Purpose

We get so caught up in day-to-day living, that sometimes we forget that we have a special purpose. We are so caught up in earning money and making a living, we forget about living our lives. We forget about what is really important in life. We become so worldly that we forget there is so much more to life than work, money, fame and fortune. Life offers us so much more when we can pause and pay attention to what life's lessons are for us. When we are living our purpose, the other things will be added unto us. Our purpose will bring the fortune and fame we seek. It may not come the way we think it should, but it will come when we are living our purpose.

I am a perfect example of that. I have worked in various fields and earned lots of money in most. But, until I started speaking, and became passionate about it, I was simply earning money. Now I am creating a life. I love what I do and I do it well. I no longer have the message, the message has me. But, before you can discover your passion in life, you have to examine your life to see where you are right now, and what you need to do to get where you want to go.

Some people live lives of boredom and mediocrity because they don't have any goals or dreams. They are wandering, aimlessly. Getting up every day and going to bed every night, and not accounting for what goes on in between. This person will wake up one day with her life spent, nothing to show for her time on earth. What a sad state of affairs. This does not have to be. We can all dream and have those dreams come true, if we dare to dream big dreams and then go to work to make those dreams a reality.   *...Dream the impossible* *dream...Reach for the unreachable star...No matter how hopeless... No matter how far.*

Some of us have forgotten how to dream. We have had so many things happen to us in life that we have forgotten how to dream. The ability to dream about what you want to do today, tomorrow, or even five years from now, is an important step in achieving success. Too few people take time to get in touch with their dreams or even stop long enough to think about what they are or what they want. Remember if you can dream it, it is possible that you can have it. Don't allow past failures to stop you from dreaming big. Think of something that seems almost impossible, but because you believe you can do it, you can dream about it, you can eventually have it.

We are not here by accident. We have a purpose and a reason for being. We are masters of our fate. All we need to do is bring all our thoughts and actions into line with the creative purpose for our lives. We need only to align our thinking with our purpose. But in order to do this we have to have faith; we have to believe in our own inner guidance. We have to believe we can, before we will ever try. Answer the questions at the end of the chapter. Really think about the answers. The answers hold the key to your purpose in life.

EXERCISE

Finding Your Purpose

Spend some quiet time thinking about what it is you want from life. You are never too young or too old to think seriously about your life. Thinking positively about your life helps you understand that there is a purpose for your life. Purpose gives our lives meaning, and having meaningful lives motivates us to do well.

The more we know about ourselves, the better equipped we are to make decisions about what we want to do with our lives, both personally and professionally. Answer the following questions and write the answers in your journal:

1. What do I stand for?
2. What am I good at?
3. What are my goals? Ambitions? Accomplishments?
4. What am I thankful for?
5. What are my greatest talents?
6. What do I love to do?
7. What gives me the greatest joy?
8. What is unique about me?
9. What do I want to accomplish before I die?
10. What is my life mission as I perceive it right now? (This may change over the years, but what do you perceive as your life mission right now?)

The keys to what you really want are oftentimes the things you don't like to admit. For example: "I don't like to admit it but, I like to be the center of attention. Ok, so go out and find a career that will let you show off. Some jobs that let you show off are: acting, teaching, speaking, dancing, comedian, magician, athlete, etc.

1. I don't like to admit it but, (fill in the blank)

_____

_____

_____

2. If I could have any kind of job, what would it be?

_____

_____

_____

3. Of all the people I know, or have seen or read about, whose job would I most like to have?

_____

_____

_____

Success is A 4 Letter Word—G O A L

I remember an experience I had recently, when I was looking at the personal goals I had written two years earlier. I was startled to discover that I had accomplished every single one of them. I also became astutely aware of my attitude about success. I always saw myself not as successful, but as *"striving"* for success. I never saw myself as, nor accepted the fact that I was, successful. Startled by this revelation, I decided to look at my current goal sheet and discovered that I had achieved ¾ of the goals on that sheet and the year was still 3 months from being over. If I stayed on course, I would achieve my goals for this year, also. Why am I sharing this with you? Because I have met lots of people, especially women, who are a lot like me. Most of us measure success by how much money we make. And, if we fall short of that dollar amount, we discount the other accomplishments. Well, I am proud to say I have changed that attitude. I hope you will, too. Success comes first, the money comes later. Sometimes much later. Just ask any successful person you know. I am successful because I have achieved my goals. I looked at my life and realized it had changed significantly, for the better. I am a national, motivational speaker traveling all over the country. I have produced a successful audio cassette series, *How To Change Your Life* and authored this book *Loving Yourself First*. I host one of the top-rated, radio talk shows in Los Angeles, *The Motivation Power Hour*. I have toured for 3 years with the largest and most successful women's conferences in the world, *The African American Women On Tour (AAWOT)*.   I have a working relationship with the greatest motivational speaker in the country, Les Brown, my mentor and my friend; and his wife, world-renowned vocalist, Gladys Knight. I have a husband who loves me and supports my dream, and a family who is my greatest source of inspiration. I have all of this and more, and I did not realize I was successful. Why? because I was not giving myself permission to enjoy the journey. Success is a journey and we should learn to enjoy it along the way. It is the journey, not the destination that gives us the greatest joy.

I am successful, are you? Are you not allowing yourself to feel successful, because you have not made all the money you think you should? Are you using the phraseology, *"When I become successful...?"* Success is a 4 letter word—**G O A L**. When we set goals, write them down, create a plan of action with time lines, and go to work to achieve them, we are successful. Because your success is as important to me as my own, I am giving an exercise at the end of this chapter to help you write and achieve your goals. Enjoy the journey.

After reading this, and understanding your beliefs about yourself, I hope you can make a commitment to allow yourself to enjoy your accomplishments, achieve your goals, create the life you want and claim your success. Do not allow money to be the only measure of your success.

Note: You may think this is a lot of work and it is. I didn't say it was going to be *easy* or *effortless*. I said it would be *worth it*. Only you can decide whether you are worth the effort.

Exercise

List all the reasons you are successful, other than money. Money is important, but so are all the other things that come with success. Example: achievement, recognition, acquired skills, living your dreams, sharing with loved ones, etc.

I am successful because:

_____

_____

_____

_____

_____

How To Set and Achieve Your Goals

We are going to look at three areas of goal setting: Personal Development (who you are committed to becoming, emotionally, mentally, physically, spiritually), Material Goals (cars, vacations, etc.) and Financial Goals.

Take a blank sheet of paper, write as fast as you can. Keep the pen moving for **ten minutes.** Write down anything that you would like to develop in your life. Anything you would like to do, be, or have. What would you like to master? What are your career goals? Social goals? Spiritual goals? Get creative. What fears do you want to conquer? What weight or energy level would you like to achieve?

Goals are dreams with a deadline. Purpose is stronger than objects. Go through each goal and put a time line on it. Next to each goal, put a one if it's something you're committed to accomplishing in the next year or less. A three, if you'll achieve it in the next three years; a five for five years; a 10 for 10 years or less, and 20 for 20 years or less. You may not know how you will achieve these goals, but that's not important right now.

Go through the list of personal development goals, and select your top three one-year goals that you are absolutely committed to achieving within the next year. Then write a paragraph as to **why** you are absolutely committed to achieving this goal within the next year. Reasons come first, answers come second. So your reason should be strong enough to compel you to achieve your goals. If not, you either need stronger reasons or better goals.

Material Goals-anything you would like to have, do, or create in your life in the next year to 20 years. Many of these may have nothing to do with personal development. They can concern pure pleasure. That's OK. Think like a kid again, and let your imagination run wild. Anything at all you would like to have, write it down.

Go one by one, write down when you are absolutely committed to having these things. Within one year, three years, five years, ten years, twenty years. Don't worry about the how; concentrate on whether or not you are absolutely committed to making these goals happen.

Go through this list and look at the things one-year or less, and pick the top three one-year **material** goals and write a paragraph as to why you are absolutely committed to having these in your life. How will they make you feel? Who can you share them with? How much fun will they create for you?

Create your ultimate **financial goals**--monthly, annual, net worth in your life-time, investments, savings, college fund, real estate, mutual funds--anything related to finances, write it down. Take your one year financial goals and write down why you are absolutely committed to making them happen.

What have we accomplished so far? Let's review. You now have a list of goals you are absolutely committed to achieving, and you have the timeline for achieving them. You know why you want them and that's the power. **How would you feel if all your one-year goals were attained?** You should be thoroughly inspired and motivated to achieve them.. If you are, you will achieve them. If not, you need better goals.

Take your top priority, one year goals, and your why for achieving them, and put them someplace where you can see them every day. Of course, your next step will be to develop an action plan. A step by step plan for achieving your one-year goals.

Whatever the first step is do that as soon as possible. For example: If your goal was to lose 20 pounds in 6 months, your first step may be to contact a gym or a nutritionist, or weigh yourself and take your measurements, or set up an exercise schedule, or whatever you determine that first step to be. Then your write out step two, three, four, etc. **Remember: goals without action are wishes.**

Chapter 10

Living The Life You Deserve

Get excited about who you are. About your life and the possibilities for your life. Don't wait for someone else to excite you; excite yourself. When you know what the possibilities are for your life, you can't help but get excited. It's when we don't know what the possibilities are that we lose our zest for living. It's when we have not taken the time to know who we are and what we are capable of that we feel life is worthless. Our lives have meaning. All life has meaning. I get so excited about all the wonderful things that can happen in a lifetime. Look at all the wonderful things in our world. It is when we focus on the negatives of life that we become disillusioned. Don't focus on the negatives. Focus your energies and efforts on the positive. Life can be a positive experience. It is how we choose to live our lives that determine whether life is a positive or a negative experience. We can choose every minute of every day whether that minute is going to be positive or negative. I am not naive. I know things happen in life that are out of our control, and they are not always positive. Death, divorce, illness, job loss, etc. When these kinds of things happen to us, we often feel there is nothing we can do. We cannot change the situation, but we can always choose how we are going to react or respond to it. If it gets us down temporarily, we can decide for how long, and we have the power and the will to come back over and over again. We can be resilient. Sometimes, life will hand us something we feel is too much. We may feel overwhelmed or inadequate. This is understandable. The problem is so often people give up. They stop trying. They become cynical, and they develop that *"what's the use, nothing ever works out anyway"* attitude. None of us want to experience disappointment and failure. But, disappointment and failure are a part of life. What we have to do is learn how to respond to these negative situations. We do that by changing our beliefs and changing our actions.

The first step is to change your belief or your perception that nothing ever works out for you. When you make a statement like that, what you are saying is, it did not work in the past and it will not work in the future. When you take on that attitude, you are setting yourself up for failure. You are limiting your future based on your past. If you don't believe it will work out, are you going to try? Probably not. And if you try, you will not give it your best. Why should you, it won't work anyway. Do you see how this becomes a vicious cycle? So you have to focus on what you can do today to make things better. The greatest secret for handling our grievances, our failures, our disappointments, is to release them. Clear them out of your mind. Refuse to think of them as having any power over you, any place in the present or any part of your future. They are part of the past; leave them there. If we look back over all of our past experiences, we may discover that everything has happened for the best. Forget the mistakes you have made and the failures you have experienced. The past is gone forever. The only place it can exist is in our minds, our memories, and in our heads. If we are intelligent, we look for the cause and profit by the experience. We take what we have learned to create a better present and future for ourselves. Mistakes are a part of life. We all make them. But, we have to be able to move past them and get on with our lives. Do not, under any circumstances, allow them to control you, to control your actions or your life.

The second thing we have to do is control what we do, our actions. The worst thing we can do is to do nothing. But when we have feelings of failure and disappointment, we become depressed and we do nothing. Depression stops you from taking the very action that could change your life. How do we bring ourselves out of it? By changing our focus. Focus on what is possible, instead of what is impossible. Focus on the present, not the past. Focus on the actions you can take today, no matter how small, that can move you closer to achieving your goal.

I have interviewed hundreds of successful people. They all say the same thing. The difference between people who fail, and people who succeed, is **persistence.** The ability to hang in there when the going gets tough. The ability to work through challenges without giving up. The ability to stay until the job is done. Success is seldom quick and never easy. So it is your ability to persist that makes the difference. It is your commitment to never give up, never quit, no matter how difficult the challenge, no matter how impossible the dream, no matter how great the odds. The only thing that matters is your willingness to persist until you succeed. How many people have that kind of determination? All successful people have it. The good news is you can have it, too. Decide what is important to you. What it is you want to accomplish.

What is it that you want to have or to be? Now, determine what the actions are that you need to take and start today taking action and keep taking action. Find ways to increase the amount of action you take.

Take deliberate, consistent, action every day. If what you are doing is not working, try something new. Repeat this affirmation three times a day. *I will persist until I succeed.*

Examine Your Life

*The unexamined life is not worth living...*That is a saying I have heard for years, without really understanding fully what it meant. But, now I truly understand it's meaning. If we are going recklessly through life, not stopping to examine our actions, thoughts or deeds, we are living an unexamined life, and it is only a matter of time before we self-destruct.

When we examine our lives, we open ourselves up for criticism. We are taking a risk, a chance of seeing something we may not like. But, when we examine our lives, we also open ourselves up for change, for improvement, for growth. We become clear about what we need to do. To examine means to take a closer look, to identify what is happening right now, to give ourselves a check-up, to contemplate, to evaluate, to take an assessment. So make sure you are living a well-examined life.

Take note of what is going on in your life. Is it what you want? If it is not, do you realize that you have the power to change it? It surprises me how many people are unhappy with their lives, but believe they have no choice but to continue living lives they hate. They don't seem to understand that they are responsible for getting what they want.

So many people go through life aimlessly. Never making any commitments to themselves or to anything worthwhile and they wonder why they have uncommitted, unfulfilled, unsuccessful lives. They are wandering through life without commitment, without any idea of where they are going and why they are here.

We must at some point become fully responsible for our actions. We must be willing to take responsibility for what we want to happen in our lives and stop blaming others for what is not taking place in our lives.

EXERCISE

Answer the following questions.   Write the answers in your journal.

What are you willing to do to change your own life?
What are you willing to sacrifice to make sure you can lead the kind of life you want?
What are you willing to give up?
What are you willing to invest in?
What are you willing to become in order to live the kind of life you want to live?

Make a list of your Wants, Dreams and/or Fantasies.   Be as specific as you can.   Can you see it, feel it, touch it, hear it? Allow your imagination to take over.

 1.
 2.
 3.
 4.
 5.

Dream, Dream, Dream (pretend that money and training are not an issue.) Select one of your dreams and create a paragraph answering the following questions.   Add any information that will help you see your dream as real.   Close your eyes and imagine having achieved your dream.   Think about how you would feel right now if your dream were a reality.

How would you walk? Talk?
Where would you live?

How would you dress?
What would you drive?
Who would you be around?
How would your life change?

Distinguish Yourself

Dare to be different. Don't do something simply because everyone else is doing it. You don't have to wear designs you don't like, or that don't flatter your figure, because some fashion designer says its the style. The bold among us go where no woman has ever gone before and leaves a trail. Once you know who you are, you know your strengths and weaknesses, you know what your values are, your greatest desires, once you love yourself fully and unconditionally, it is easy to distinguish yourself. It becomes easier to not follow the crowd, to stand on your own principles and stand up for what you believe, even if it is not the popular belief.

To distinguish yourself from the crowd takes guts. Those that have the courage are the leaders in every field you can think of. They have a vision and a dream for their lives that transcend what others think or say. They believe in themselves, and they have faith that what they want will become a reality. Because they believe, they work hard to make it a reality. They are willing to take risks. They are willing to risk failure. They are willing to stretch and grow. They are willing to take the disappointments and turn them into victories. They refuse to give up even in the face of great adversity. They look at their challenges as opportunities to grow. They learn from their mistakes, they take the lessons learned from them and continue to move forward. You can do the same thing if you have the courage to try.

When you distinguish yourself from the crowd, you open yourself up for criticism and ridicule from those who do not understand your dream. You risk rejection, may even lose some friends, but you will gain others. I believe there is no gain without some risk. We have to be willing to risk what we have for what we want. If we are talking about our goals, our dreams, our lives, it is not that big of a risk. It is probably a bigger risk not to try. We lose more by not trying than we do by trying and failing. Because if we try and fail, at least we can look for the lesson. If we learn the lesson, we profit by our mistakes. Profiting by our mistakes means that we will not repeat the same ones twice.

Be willing to distinguish yourself. Recognize your talents and work tirelessly to develop them. That is the only way you will be truly happy. We distinguish ourselves by knowing what we want and going after it. By being our own person and not following the crowd because it is the popular thing to do. We distinguish ourselves by setting goals and working tirelessly to achieve them. We distinguish ourselves by setting the pace instead of following in the steps of others. By competing with ourselves to become better rather than looking at what others are doing and comparing ourselves to them. We are distinguished when we realize that God gave us a free will and we can use that will to create whatever we want in life.

Loving yourself, respecting yourself and valuing yourself gives your life power and purpose. Distinguishing yourself will help you achieve that purpose. It is easier to distinguish yourself when you know what your purpose is and you are pursuing it. There is less resistance and things go so much smoother.

Most people fail in life not because they prepare to fail but they fail to prepare. They never make preparation for success. They don't expect to succeed, therefore they don't. But, you can succeed because you have the formula. Step away from the crowd. 95% of the people you meet don't know their purpose. They don't know where they are going. They don't know their way. They do not have written, well-defined goals. It is easy to distinguish yourself simply by deciding what you want, writing it down in the form of goals and creating an action plan to achieve those goals. That puts you in the top 5% of the people.

To distinguish yourself further, go after what you want. Most people, even when they know what they want, never take action. Take action. Do something everyday that takes you closer to achieving your goal. Be consistent and persistent. Find unconventional ways to market yourself. If you can't be the first, be the best. If you can't be the best, create something you can be first in (first rule of marketing). Don't try to blend in or be like everybody else. We have discussed knowing yourself throughout this book. Know your strengths. If you know yourself, you can distinguish yourself by utilizing your strength and your uniqueness.

Improving Your Risk Taking Skills

Don't be afraid to take risks. It is almost impossible to succeed without taking some risks. If you are not comfortable taking risks, you are not alone. Lots of women are afraid of taking risks.   But, almost without exception, the most successful people have learned how to take calculated risks. You, too, can learn risk-taking skills.

How good are you at taking risks? In a study of 100 men and women, it was found that women had **learned** to **view** risk-taking **negatively**, while men had **learned** to **weigh** its **potential** for **negative** and **positive** results. It is important to **develop** a **positive approach** to risk-taking.

To Achieve your goals, both lifetime and immediate, to make things happen in your life, you must be willing to take a risk. But to be effective, you must enhance your ability to take risks rationally and appropriately.   To be effective, you need a positive attitude toward risk taking that allows you to learn and grow.

To build such an attitude, you must: ask yourself what you might **gain**—as well as **lose** by taking a risk. Determine how the risk might effect your long-term personal and professional goals. Become fully aware of the facts surrounding the risk. Increase the number of well-thought out, calculated risks you take.   Develop confidence in your ability to deal with the results and learn from the experience. Whether it is a risk in your personal or professional life, the idea is a plan. Planning reduces your anxiety and increases your chance of success.

Risk can be categorized into high, moderate, low. The level at which you view risk depends on you. What is high for one person may be moderate or low for another. Are you so afraid of losing you won't take any risk, regardless of the level, or are you always jumping in without knowing the level of the risk? Answer the questions in the exercise portion of this chapter to help you determine where you are as a risk-taker, to help improve your risk-taking skills, and to help you create a plan for taking rational, appropriate risks.

Becoming comfortable with risk-taking and, enhancing your ability to take risks, will distinguish you even further. It was my risk taking-skills that enabled me to develop my radio talk show without prior radio experience. To leave the profession of real estate and finance after fifteen years to become a full time motivational speaker. To write this book. Each of these ventures carried with it a certain amount of risk.

Anything worth doing in life requires that we take a risk. It is so very important to your success that you must not skip over this chapter. Answer the questions at the end of the chapter. Take your time because you will be able to identify your risk-taking habits. Maybe you have not taken enough risks in your life and need to take more. Perhaps, you have been too risky, too careless and need to learn to take well thought out, calculated risks. Only you can decide that by answering the questions and applying the information you learn from the answers.

EXERCISE.

Answer the following questions to determine how to distinguish yourself from the crowd:

What is unique or different about me?
How can I best display or present that uniqueness or difference?

Am I a risk-taker? _____yes _____no
Regardless of your answer to this question, continue:

Identifying your personal approach to taking risks is the first step towards understanding and improving your abilities in this area. Answer these questions:

1. How do I perceive risk?
2. What risks have I taken that are low, moderate high?
3. Where were my feelings before, during and after the risk?
4. What did I gain? What did I lose?
5. What options did I consider?
6. What else should I have considered?

Planning is an important part of risk-taking. It organizes the process into manageable steps and reduces your anxiety and increases your willingness to continue taking rational, appropriate risks. List a risk you are either currently facing, or anticipate facing in the near future, and answer these questions:

1. What level of risk is it? (low, moderate or high?)

2. What do I want the results to be?
3. What concerns do I have about taking this risk?
4. What will I gain, lose, if I take this risk?
5. How can I minimize my losses?
6. What are my options?
7. How can I move the risk from high to moderate?

Write out a plan of action based on your answers to the above questions.

Believe In Yourself and Have Faith

If you don't believe in yourself, who will? Believe you can do whatever you make up your mind to do. Don't live in past failures. Look for the lesson in the failure. Maybe there was something you needed to learn and you could not learn it any other way. Perhaps you are hardheaded, and need to learn through failure. Get the lesson and move on. Believe that you are going to be able to do whatever it is you want to do.

Believing in yourself also requires that you know and appreciate your weaknesses, as well as your strengths. That you build on your strengths. All of us have strengths and weaknesses. Most people dwell on their weaknesses. They think about what they can't do rather that what they can do. You can increase your belief in yourself by focusing on your strengths. We need to be aware of our weaknesses, but they should not be the focus. Focus on what can be instead of what can't be.

Belief in yourself creates opportunity. When we believe we can do something we try harder, we are willing to do more. Because we are willing to do more, we create opportunities for ourselves. We can see things other people can't. Opportunities are created out of hard work and preparation.

Belief in oneself is essential to success. When we believe in ourselves, we have the courage to try new things, to take risks, to fail and get up and keep trying. When we believe in ourselves, we do not allow other people's opinions to stop us. We are not looking to others to validate us. We are not seeking permission or acceptance from others. We are more concerned with our own opinion.

But, believing in yourself requires that you know yourself. That you love and appreciate who you are. That you continue to learn and grow. It requires that you be realistic about who you are and totally unrealistic about who you can become. Dream big dreams, then go to work to make them a reality. Develop faith in yourself and in your dreams. We do that by reaffirming ourselves and our dreams. Using affirmations, visualization and prayer. Prayer is an excellent way of affirming. It connects us with the spirit. Prayer validates our faith. Faith is knowing something will happen. Faith is seeing your dream, before it ever becomes a reality. Faith is knowing in your heart that it will come true. In the bible Paul said *Faith is the ability to call forth those things as though they were.* We call forth those things through prayer.

We tend to put our faith in everything but ourselves. We look to other people, television, movies, magazines, drugs, alcohol, everything but ourselves. We cherish our delusions, fool ourselves into believing we are not so bad. We refuse to look problems and challenges square in the face. We refuse to have faith and confidence in our own abilities to solve the problem. The bible says *if we have faith as a grain of mustard seed.* Do you know how small a grain of mustard seed is? About the size of the head of a needle. You can barely see it with the naked eye. But, if we have just a little faith, we can change our lives. We are not talking religion here. We are talking about your beliefs, and using those beliefs to strengthen your faith and your belief in yourself.

To create belief and confidence, start with something small. When you accomplish that, try something harder. Small accomplishments create confidence and help us believe we really can do it. Try new and different things. You don't have to be good at all of them. Do something just for the fun of doing it. All of this builds self-confidence. Helps us believe in ourselves. Makes it ok to not do something well. Makes it ok to not know, but to be willing to learn. Be open to the things that you really love doing. Self-confidence comes from doing, and doing creates the belief that we can accomplish what we want to. Believing in ourselves and having faith are the two most powerful tools we possess, and we can use these tools to help us love ourselves unconditionally. We can use these tools to help us see our talents and accomplish our goals. If we have faith in ourselves, and in a power greater than ourselves, we can do anything. *All things are possible to he that believeth.* Make a commitment to your life. Unless we are committed we find all kinds of excuses for not doing what we need to do. Commitment is the key to accomplishment.

So, now that we know we have the power, what are we going to do with it? I know some people spend their whole lives never realizing they have this kind of power. You are blessed because you know something 95% of the people in the world don't seem to know. What are you going to do about it? Are you going to continue to be miserable, unhappy, dissatisfied, or are you going to take responsibility for your own life? Are you going to continue to blame, or are you going to do something about it? Are you going to wait for someone or something to come along and give you what you need, or are you going to go out and find it? It is your choice.

Start every morning by affirming your faith in a higher power, in yourself, and in the universe. Know that this higher power is ever present within you. Know that you have everything that you need to be successful in this life. Know that everything in the universe belongs to you. Know that you and the universe are one. Know that the laws of the universe are created for your good, and by knowing these laws, you increase your chances of success. The laws are unchanging and unwavering. If you give, you must receive. If you sow, you will reap. If you plant love, you get love. If you plant hate, you get hate. For every cause there is an effect. There is an ebb and a flow. There is a time to plant and a time to harvest. Light follows the darkness. It has not come to stay, but to pass. If the only laws we follow are man-made laws, we are going to suffer great consequences. Always ask yourself, *"What is the law?"* Not man-made law, but the law of nature. Are you trying to work against it? When we work against the laws of man, we feel it in our outer lives. When we work against the law of nature, we feel the discomfort in our bodies, in our inner lives.

Keep your faith alive through meditation and prayer. Spend some quiet time. Know what it is that you want, and do something every day to move you closer to your goals. Spend quality time on quality projects and with quality people. Don't sell yourself short. Know that you can have whatever you want in life if you are willing to become the person deserving of it. You can get it through shortcuts and deceit, but you will get all the ills that go along with that kind of life style. No peace, always afraid someone is going to take what you have away. In my opinion that is too high a price to pay.

You are reading this book so you are searching for the right thing to do. You have decided that the other way is not for you. You are searching for the inner peace we can all have by maintaining faith in that higher power, and in ourselves. An unwavering faith. A faith that carries us through the rough times to the good times that we are so deserving of. Have faith in yourself, and the world will open up to you. Have faith in goodness, and your life will reflect that. Have faith that there is a higher power and an everlasting life, and you will flourish in this life. Have faith that all the universe was created for you, and you will never feel poverty even if you don't have a dime in your pocket. It is impossible to feel poverty when the universe belongs to you. The flowers, the birds, the trees, they all belong to you. The sun, the moon, the stars, they all belong to you. The ocean, the mountains, the sky, it all belongs to you. How can you feel anything but powerful knowing that the universe belongs to you and no one can ever take it away? Learn to let go of material things that bring temporary feelings of power, and reach out to those things that are unchanging for a sense of real power.

This world was created for us. No one can change that. Man can take credit for improving it or destroying it, but he cannot take credit for creating it. If you have faith, this should really make you feel powerful. This is your world and no one on earth can take it away from you. You have the power of the stars, the sun, the moon, the whole universe. Do you feel the power of ownership? Do you understand that you are a part of all of this? Do you know that you are as much a part of the universe as the sun, the moon and the stars? Do you know that there is a purpose for your life, as important as the purpose for the sun, the moon and the stars? Do you know that you are God's greatest creation? Do you know that God didn't make any junk? Develop faith in yourself and a power higher than yourself.

You can create the life you want by knowing your own value and recognizing that value. You are more valuable than diamonds, than gold, than jewels. You are more valuable than the oldest antique in the world. You are valueless, priceless, irreplaceable. You are the greatest creation on earth. Nothing has been able to duplicate that value since the beginning of time. You are distinctly different from every other creature on earth. You are unique and you are special. You must know this in order to have faith in yourself and your own abilities.

Having faith in yourself simply means that you believe that you are the greatest story ever written. That you believe that you are God's greatest creation. That you believe in your own worth as a human being. That you believe there is a power greater than you or I. That you believe you are as important to the universe as the sun, the moon, the stars. That you believe there is a purpose for your life and you have the ability to fulfill that purpose. That you believe in yourself in all your splendor and glory. That you believe that you can accomplish more than you have ever accomplished before. That there is still something inside you that separates you from all other animals on earth. That you have the power within you to direct and control your own life. That you came here equipped with everything you need. That there is nothing lacking except acknowledgment that your power exists and the courage to go forward. Have faith in yourself and a power greater than yourself and the world will open up for you and to you. Have faith and share that faith every chance you get, not by saying it, but by living it.

EXERCISE

Make a list of your strengths. Things you do well. We are not just talking about physical strengths, but character strengths also, such as courage, honesty, determination, etc. Write them down and read this list every time you are reminded of your weaknesses, faults or mistakes.

1.
2.
3.
4.
5.
6.
7.
8.
9.
10.

Meditation and/or Prayer

Spend some quiet time (early morning or late night, before anyone else is up or after everyone goes to bed). Close your eyes. You can count backwards from 100, or you can play soothing music, or whatever helps you relax and meditate. Relax as much as possible without going to sleep. Meditation relieves stress and helps to clarify our thinking. Think about your life and how you would like to change it. Think about what it would be like if you had already made the changes. How do you feel? See yourself having the personality qualities necessary to change your life. Example: courage, determination, enthusiasm, commitment, decisiveness, energy, intelligence, etc.

Give thanks for everything you already have. Focus on all the good things you have in your life. Being thankful for what we already have allows our blessings to expand. Following is my spiritual prayer. Use whatever spiritual prayers you have. This is simply a time for thanksgiving.

In The Spirit

I am a spiritual being. I know greater is the power within me than the power that is in the world. I know that I and the father are one. I know that I have free will to think and do and say whatever I want and I know with that will comes a big responsibility. I accept that responsibility. I yield myself to the creator. I know that the spirit is always there and I can always tap into it. It is my source of strength. My guiding light. I am never alone. I will never be deserted. I open myself up to receive all the good that life offers. I do not judge myself or other people. I release all guilt and shame from my life. I forgive myself for any wrongs and know that in the spirit I am also forgiven. I am thankful for what I already have in my life, and through prayer and thanksgiving, the good is multiplied in my life.

Create A Zest For Life

Get excited about life. You have to have a zest for life in order to endure the hardships. Life is not always easy, but it is always good if you know that the hard times are not here to stay. We are going to have challenges, but that is how we grow and develop. We have challenges so that we don't get complacent. So that we continue to move forward and not take life for granted. When we have a zest for life, when we truly love life and living the hard times won't seem so hard. We will have more good than bad. .We can create a zest for life by being grateful for everything we have. Give thanks constantly for all the good that you have in your life. Know that you deserve the best that life has to offer. Expect the best and you tend to get the best. Don't sell yourself short. Don't settle for less than you deserve. The harder you work, the luckier you are.

You and I know that what appears to be luck is hard work being revealed. So maintain your zest for life. Do something different. Something you have never done before. Get outside of your little box of boredom. Live a little. Find something you can get excited about. Keep looking ahead. Live in the present. Do not bring yesterday's problems into today unless you are prepared to solve them with today's solutions. Live in the moment because that is really all we have. Yesterday is gone and tomorrow is not promised. If you find yourself living in the past, or living for tomorrow try to turn that around right now. Today, this moment, the present is all there is. What are you prepared to do with it? Are you wasting it on wishes for yesterday or promises for tomorrow?

Today is what you make of it. Look at it as a canvas; you are the artist. you can paint whatever picture you want. But, remember whatever you paint is your life. You will have to suffer the burden of failure or the joy of success. It is your choice. It is always your choice. Decide right now, today, which you want. It can happen for you just as it has happened for thousands of others. You have to believe it can happen and then go to work to make sure it will happen. Wishing will do you no good. You have to be prepared to act. Action is the difference between having your dreams and not having your dreams. Action is the key. We can want our dreams, we can dream our dreams. We can know what we want and why we want it, but if we never do anything to achieve it, our dream will always be just a dream, a wish, a whim.

Action is the only thing standing between us and our dream. Grab that zest for life. Get excited. Go after what you want. You can learn whatever you need to learn to do whatever you want to do along the way. There is always some one that will help you when you take action. When you are doing everything you can, the universe moves in your favor. Things start to happen. I can't explain it. But, it never fails. Talk to people about what you want to do. Talk to people who will support you. If you have a dream, you need a team. A team that believes in you and your dream. A team that is willing to work with you until your dream becomes a reality. No one can be successful by themselves. We all need help, ask for it. Ask people who can and are willing to help you. But, make sure you are doing all you can. Fate favors the person who is hard at work on a worthy purpose. A person with a goal in her heart and mind. Heaven and earth seems to move for this kind of person. You can become this kind of person by believing in yourself and your dreams. By working consistently and diligently to make them a reality. Success is not a matter of luck, but of pre-determined, conscious, consistent action. Success is easy when you know what to do. Action is the key. If we never do anything we will never be anything and we will never have anything. So take well-calculated risks. Think about what it is you want to do. Write down your goals and create a plan of action for achieving them. You are in charge. You can do whatever you choose. But, do something, anything. I believe the wrong decision is sometimes better than no decision. Start where you are, with what you have, and never give up. Do not take no for an answer. These are the characteristics of all successful people.

If you get excited, and you harness that excitement to a purpose, and you hook that purpose to a plan, and you put that plan into action and you integrate that action with faith and belief, you can do whatever you want to do and be excited about the prospects of your life. Excitement generates energy called enthusiasm. Enthusiasm creates excitement. The possibilities are endless. Never lose your excitement for life. The zest for living. It is created through our dreams and maintained by the realization of those dreams. That is why it is so important to have dreams, goals, ambitions. We can use our dreams, goals and ambitions to help maintain that zest for life. We will enjoy life well into our golden years. I certainly hope something you read on the pages of this book can make a difference in your life. The time and effort spent writing this book will be worth it, if it can serve as a catalyst to change one life. Share it with someone you care about. Encourage the men in your life to read it also. Explain to them how loving yourself first can help you love them better.

Resources

Hot Lines

AIDS	800 342-2437
	800 922-AIDS
AIDS Info. Line Countrywide	800 3396993
Domestic Violence	800 288-3845
Missing & Neglected Children	800 843-5678
Child Find of America, Inc.	800 I AM LOST
Youth Crisis	800 448-4663
Runaways (Suicide Hotline for Teens)	800 621-4000

Suicide Prevention Hotline   800 242-4026

Cancer Information   800 422-6237

American Cancer Society   800 ACS-2345

Parents Anonymous   800 352-0386

Elder Abuse   800 992-1660

Cocaine   800 Cocaine

Professional Organizations

National Association of Women Business Owners
NAWBO - Los Angeles
1804 W. Burbank Blvd.
Burbank, Ca. 91506-1315

Coalition for Women's Economic Development (CWED)
315 W. Ninth St., Suite 705
Los Angeles, Ca. 90015
(213) 489-4995
Assist low-income women with self-employment

National Council of Negro Women (NCNW)
P. O. Box 90960
Washington, D. C. 20077-7366
Dorothy I. Height, National President

National Association for Female Executives
1(800) 636-6233 ext 192

African American Women On Tour (AAWOT)
3914 Murphy Canyon Road, Suite 216
San Diego, California 92123
(619) 560-2770/(619) 560-9190 Fax
Maria Carothers, Executive Director

Professional Women In Business
Networking Systems (PWIB)
20220 S. Avalon Blvd., Ste. 188
Carson, California 90746
(310) 669-4723
Corliss Tillman, Founder/President

MTI
Professional Automotive Consulting For Women
13337 E. South Street, Suite 232
Cerritos, California 926-5008
Mary Taylor
Professional automotive consulting for women

American Society of Association Executives (ASAE)
1575 Eve Street, NW
Washington, D. C. 20005-1168
(202) 626-2803/(202) 371-8825 Fax

California American Woman's Economic Development
Corporation (AWEB)
100 W. Broadway, Suite 500
Long Beach, Ca. 90802-4432
(310) 983-3747?(310) 983-3750
Orange County Office (714)474-AWEB/ (714) 474-7416 Fax
Trains women to successfully run their own business

Black Single Parents Network
7800 S. Broadway
Los Angeles, Ca.
(213) 752-9511

Black Women's Network
P. O. Box 56106
Los Angeles, Ca. 90056
(213) 964-4003

Black Women's Forum
3870 Crenshaw Blvd., Suite 210
Los Angeles, Ca. (213) 292-3009

The Women's Yellow Pages
13601 Ventura Blvd., #374
Sherman Oaks, Ca. 91423
(818)   995-6646/(714) 520-4620/(909) 467-1439

Women Incorporated
1401 21st Street, Suite 310
Sacramento, Ca. 95814
800 930-3993/(916) 448-8898 Fax
Los Angeles Office (310) 473-5787/(310) 477-7459 Fax

New York City Office (212)479-2366/ (212) 479-2549

New York Conference Office (212) 551-3571/(212) 551-3572

Service Organizations

SBA - The Office of Women's Business Ownership
The SBA has offices located throughout the United States
For the one in your area look under "U. S. Government"
or call the Small Business Answer Desk at (800) 8 ASK-SBA.
(202) 205-6673

Southern California Youth and Family Center
101 North La Brea Suite 100
Ingelwood, CA 90301
(310)671-1222

National Black Child Development Institute
Washington, D. C.
(800) 556-2234

Children's Defense Fund
P.O. Box 75086
Washington, D.C. 22013

Big Sisters of Los Angeles
6022 Wilshire Blvd., Suite 202
Los Angeles, California
(213) 933-5749

Mad Dads
Men Against Destruction Defending Against
Drugs and Social Disorder
4625 Crenshaw Blvd.
Los Angeles, Ca.
(213) 290-7111

Coalition For Substance Abuse Prevention
8500 S. Broadway
Los Angeles, Ca.
(213)   750-9087

National Black Child Development Institute
943 Stillwell Avenue
San Diego, Ca.
(619) 543-9090

California Women's Comm. on Alcohol & Drugs
Information & technical assistance
(818)   376-0470

Mothers Against Drunk Drivers (M.A.D.D.)
(818) 986-6233
Crime Victim Center-Los Angeles
Services & therapy for victims of violent crimes
(213)   857-5855

The Response Center (W.LA)
Hot line for victims of violent crimes
(310) 855-3506

Los Angeles County Dept. of Children Services
Report suspected child abuse cases
(310)   312-5225/312-5226
(Each county has their own. Get the listing in your county)

Family Services Los Angeles
(213) 381-3626

Child & Family Services - Los Angeles
Resources and Referrals
(213) 413-0777

Parents Anonymous
Parents concerned about abusing their children
(800) 352-0386 Hot line

Safe Rides Los Angeles
Safe rides for teens Fri. & Sat.
(310)   374-CARE

Missing Persons, Intl.
Missing children and adults
(805)   255-0944

L. A. Women's Foundation
Educational, Provides fund raising & financial
(213)938-9828

Black Single Parent Network
1242 E. Imperial Hwy.
Los Angeles, Ca. 90059
(213) 564-0391

Inner Visions
Spiritual Life Maintenance Network
P. O. Box 3231
Silver Spring, MD 20918-0231
Prison Ministry

National Women's Economic Alliance Foundation
Research & Education provide access to govt. & industry leaders addressing concerns impacting women in the workplace.
(202) 638-1200

Women's Prison Ministry
Assistance for women coming out of prison
(212) 464-5100

LA County Commission on the Status of Women
Women's referral service

Women's AIDs Project
(213) 650-1508

Rosa Parks Sexual Assault Crisis Center
(213)   295-8582
24 hour Sexual Assault   (213) 295-HOPE

YWCA Women's Shelter
24 hour hotline (310) 437-4663

Jenesse Center
24 hour hotline (213) 755-6836

Life Adjustment Group, Inc.
101 N. La Brea Avenue, Suite 503
Inglewood, California 90301-1792
(310) 412-1523 / (310) 330-4723
A private counseling group practice providing community based counseling services

Annointed Waters Christian Counseling Center
9132 S. Western Avenue
Los Angeles, Ca.
(213) 755-9901

The Perecon Institute For the Study of
Personal Finance and Economics
2116 Arlington Avenue, Suite 225
Los Angeles, Ca. 90017
(213) 731-2325 / 888-Perecon
Courses are absolutely free

Pacific Coast Regional Small Business Development Corp.
3255 Wilshire Blvd., Suite 1501
Los Angeles, Ca. 90010
(213) 739-2999 / (213) 739-0639 Fax
Entrepreneurial Institute

Youth Organizations

Volunteers Of America
Upward Bound/Talent Search
520 S. LaFayette Park Place, Suite 304
Los Angeles, Ca. 90057
Youth Educational Program

TET, INC. Tomorrow's Entrepreneurs Today
P. O. Box 47442
Los Angeles, Ca. 90047
(213) 964-1883?(213) 777-6524 Fax
Empowering Youth To Soar

Future Kids
Computer based learning center for kids
4119 S. Sepulveda Blvd.
Culver City, Ca. 90230-4706
(310) 572-9900/(310) 572-9904 Fax

Challengers Boys & Girls Club
5029 S. Vermont Avenue
Los Angeles, Ca.
(213) 971-6161

Newsletters

Woman To Woman "A Good News Letter"
P. O. Box 35513
Los Angeles, California 90035
Juanita Parker

The Witting Woman Newsletter
P. O. Box 6697
Santa Ana, Ca. 92706-0697
Joyanne McDaniel

Sister Speak
3914 Murphy Canyon Road, Suite 216
San Diego, California 92123
Maria Dowd Carothers

Suggested Reading

Being A Woman
Dr. Toni Grant
Avon Books, NY

Repackage Yourself
Corliss Tillman
M Systems - Publishing Group

*Get Out of Your Own Way: Overcoming Self
Defeating Behavior*
Dr. Mark Goulston
Perigee Publishing

Women Who Love Too Much
Robin Norwood
Pocket Books NY

Ten Stupid Things Women Do To Mess up Their Lives
Dr. Laura Schlessinger
HarperPerennial,
A Division of Harper Collins Publishers

Satisfying The Black Man Sexually
Dr. Rosie Milligan
Professional Business Consultant

In The Company of My Sisters
Julia A. Boyd
Dutton Publishers

Faith In The Valley
Iyanla VanZant
Simon & Schuster New York

Value In The Valley
Iyanla VanZant
Simon & Schuster New York

In The Spirit
Susan Taylor
Amistad Press, Inc. NY

How To Find A BMW (Black Man Working)
Dr. Julia Hare
The Black Think Tank, S. F., CA

Talking With Teens In Turbulent Times
John Alston
Longmeadow Press

Laws Of Success
Napoleon Hill
Success Unlimited, Inc.

The Personal Touch
Terrie Williams
Warner Books

Living With Your Teenage Daughter and Liking It
Meryl Fishman & Kathleen Horwich
Simon & Shuster NY

Overcoming Doubt, Fear & Procrastination
Barbara Wright Sykes
Collins Publications

Think It Do It
The Procrastinators Guide to Action
Nina Craft, Ph.D.

Sacred Pampering Principles
Debrena Jackson Gandy
William Morrow & Co.

How To Love A Black Man
Dr. Ronn Elmore
Warner Books

Talking Dollars and Making Sense
Brooke Stephens
McGraw Hill

The Start Of Something Big
(Everything You Must Know to be Successful
In Your Own Business)
Kimberly L. Johnson
Noted Concepts S. D., Ca.

Do You Want Profits or Paychecks
Kevin L. Smith
Way To Go Publishing

The Basic Money Management Workbook
Glinda Bridgeforth

Creating Wealth
Robert G. Allen
Simon & Schuster, Inc. New York

Success Runs In Our Race
George Fraser

Live Your Dreams
Les Brown
William Morrow & Company

It's Not Over Until You Win
Les Brown
Simon & Schuster

How To Improve Self Esteem in the African American Child
Ida Greene
P.S.I. Publishers

Richard Hittleman's Yoga
28 Day Exercise Plan
Bantam Books

About the Author

Linda Coleman-Willis is a national motivational speaker, personal development trainer, and workshop leader focusing on Leadership, Diversity, Customer Service and Team Building. She provides workshops and seminars, and is a much sought after keynote speaker for major corporations, organizations and associations.

Linda hosts a weekly radio talk show, *"The Motivation Power Hour"* where she interviews national speakers such as Les Brown, Iyanala Van Zant, George Fraser, Bertice Berry, Patricia Fripp, Brooke Stephens, Terrie Williams, and Jack Canfield, author of Chicken Soup For The Soul. Linda seems to have a knack for attracting the best and for selecting topics that sizzle. In her own words the show "educates, elevates, empowers, enlightens, entertains and excites" the listening audience to "become the very best that they can be both personally and professionally." The show can be heard every Sunday evening 7:00PM on KYPA AM 1230 Los Angeles and AM 1220 Pomona.

Linda Coleman-Willis is not just a super talk show host, but an exciting, electrifying speaker. She has excited audiences all over America. She uses stories to teach people how to overcome obstacles in their lives as she has struggled to overcome obstacles in her own life. Her dream of speaking at the Crystal Cathedral became a reality last year.

Linda can also be seen on the TV show "Making It, Minority Success Stories" providing her "Secrets of Success" on KTLA Channel 5. She works with Les Brown and Gladys Knight to promote Personal Development Television, and has spent the last four years touring with the "African American Women On Tour" conference.

Linda served as a trainer/facilitator for the Los Angeles Urban League's Speakers Bureau and Coach/Mentor for the Miss Los Angeles Beauty Pageant. She has taught personal development programs to students throughout the nation, appeared on numerous radio and TV shows and writes for several publications.

Linda's in-depth training and experience lie in the field of real estate and finance. She received her Real Estate license in 1981 and graduated with honors from the Mortgage Banking Institute with an emphasis in finance. She was a top producing sales person for eight years and a member of the distinguished "Million Dollar Club." She founded an organization "Women For Financial Independence" which earned her the honored title

"Outstanding Woman of America."   Linda worked as a Community Development Liaison for Bank of America handling all of Southern California. She owned and operated a Real Estate Firm and Mortgage Brokerage Company for five years before entering the speaking/training field and establishing LC & Associates.

Linda is a member of the National Speakers Association and a Distinguished Toastmaster. She is listed in *Who's Who In Professional Speaking* and is the winner of the National Speakers Association, Greater Los Angeles Chapter's *1995 Bronze Mike Award.* She has produced an award winning tape series entitled   *"How To Change Your Life, and Achieve the Results you Want."*

Linda has made a lifetime commitment to helping people change their lives. She especially loves working with young people. She teaches self-esteem courses for Upward Bounds and Los Angeles Police Department's Jeopardy program. Linda loves to go into the inner city schools and work with kids at risk. She has a dream of one day having a Motivational Institute in the heart of the community. An institute that teaches "Life Skills." As she so often says ,"The skills you don't learn in school, are the skills we all need to live happy, healthy, productive, fun-filled lives." "I want to teach these skills to young people and adults." "Every person deserves the opportunity to live the best life possible."

Index

HOW TO CHANGE YOUR LIFE

●●●

And Achieve The Results You Want

As you listen you will learn to:
- Create a Powerful Vision of Yourself
- Discover Empowering Beliefs That Are Necessary to Change Your Life
- Choose Your Attitude -- Control Your Destiny
- Take Action Consistently and Deliberately
- Understand and Utilize the Controlling Force That Directs Your Life

HOW TO CHANGE YOUR LIFE is a powerful audio cassette program that provides you with ideas and techniques you can use immediately to begin improving your life and moving you toward the greater success you desire. You will learn how to **Take Full Responsibility** for your life, **Develop a Winning Attitude, Find Your Purpose** and **Take Positive Action.** By listening to this tape program and applying these ideas and techniques you can virtually transform your life.

LINDA COLEMAN-WILLIS is a motivational speaker and recognized leader in the Self-Development field. She **motivates, educates** and **empowers** her audience to become the best they can be. Linda combines a practical approach with her **unique style** and **sense of humor** to involve participants in a life **changing experience.** She has taught personal development programs to students throughout the nation, has appeared on numerous radio and TV shows and currently writes on the topic "Creating Wealth" for several financial publications. Linda has been selected as one of **America's Outstanding Young Women.**

This tape program can be used by your school, group or organization as a fundraiser. It is an ideal gift for children, friends and family. To contact Linda for speaking engagements or to order this audio tape program send to: **Linda Coleman , L.C. & Associates, P.O. Box 90369 Los Angeles, CA, 90009 or call (213) 243-8258**

Name_____
Address_____
City_____ State_____ Zip_____

Cassette Purchase Price: $25.00 (ea) plus $3.00 postage & handling.
CA residents add 8.25% tax.
Qty:_____ Total Enclosed: $_____

Order Form

For additional copies of *Loving Yourself First* or the audio cassette tape program (see following page) *How to Change Your Life*, make check or money order payable to Linda Coleman and send payment to:

L.C. & Associates
P. O. Box 90369
Los Angeles, California 90009

Fill in the following information:

Name:_____

Address:_____

City:_____

State:_____   Zip:_____

Number of books required: _____: **of cassette programs**_____

Purchase Price:
$12.95 per book
$25.00 per cassette program

Sales Tax:
California addresses must pay the state sales tax of 8.25% per book.

Shipping and Handling:
Add $3.00 per book or audio cassette program for Shipping and Handling (please allow three to four weeks for shipping). For orders to be shipped via airmail add an additional $2.00 (for a total of $5.00).